PARTIES
FOR KIDS

JUDY BASTYRA

TED SMART

For two special little girls, Annalie Hertz and Lily Olsberg, in the hope that their lives will be one long party

KINGFISHER
An imprint of Kingfisher Publications Plc
New Penderel House, 283-288 High Holborn,
London WC1V 7HZ

First published in 1998 by Kingfisher Books

This edition produced for The Book People Ltd,
Hall Wood Avenue, Haydock,
St Helens WA11 9UL

2 4 6 8 10 9 7 5 3 1

British Library Cataloguing in Publication Data
A catalogue record is available from the British Library

ISBN: 0 7534 0207 6

Editors: Anne Johnson, Belinda Weber
Designer: Sarah Goodwin
Photographers: Amanda Heywood, Ray Moller
Home economists: Carol Handslip, Netty Nicholson, Jenny Stacey
Illustrator: Claire Chrystall

Contents

Introduction

Parties for Kids is an invaluable guide to organizing a truly memorable children's party, from the invitations to the going-home presents, with many ideas for theme parties, games and delicious recipes.

A party is a special event, and you should never forget this. Children look forward to their own party for ages, and count the weeks – months even – until their special moment comes. **Parties for Kids** has been written to help take some of the stress out of giving children's parties. From the first idea to the last crumb under the chair, this book will help you give your child a party to remember.

The secret of success

The secret of success, both for a good party and for your own peace of mind, is organization. In this way, you will avoid any last-minute panic. You will also be able to look at ways of saving money, perhaps by making the decorations and the going-home presents yourself. Once you've set the date of the party, there are still a number of decisions you have to make. These will depend on what will suit your child, your accommodation and your budget. The countdown at the back of the book will be especially useful to help you fit in all the preparations for the party. Here are some general points to make the party a success.

★ **Make sure everything is ready beforehand.**

★ **Be relaxed – remember this is a very special day.**

★ **Make sure you have enough helpers.**

★ **Plan more games than you need.**

★ **Make a list of who the presents are from so your child can write thank-you cards.**

★ **Have a damp cloth ready for sticky fingers.**

★ **Be prepared to deal with a mess, and have plenty of bin bags handy.**

★ **Be specific about both the starting and ending times, and restrict the time to 2–2¹⁄₂ hours.**

Coping with different ages

Every child is different, of course, but these general guidelines should come in useful.

1-year-olds: These parties are as much for the parents and grandparents as for the child. One-year-olds will probably be accompanied by an adult, so include them in your plans for tea. The birthday child will probably be more interested in the wrapping paper than the presents. Be prepared for tears – it can all be too much!

2-year-olds: This age group will still want a parent to stay. They are probably too young for organized games but usually enjoy dancing, so have lots of music and toys for them to play with. The party should last no longer than 1½ hours.

3-year-olds: Most three-year-olds will be happy to stay without their parents but you should have plenty of adults to help with hugs, loo visits and washing hands. They can play short games, especially ones with music.

4-year-olds: This is a magical party age, when children interact well with each other. They can become overexcited, though, so plan all the games carefully and don't let the party go on for too long.

5-year-olds: They can be quite self-conscious at this age and may become boisterous. Plan more games than you actually need, in case they play them more quickly than you expected. Have a few calming-down games up your sleeve, in case they become too rowdy.

6-year-olds: At this age, they are starting to develop skills such as painting, gluing and cutting, and will probably want to help you with all the preparations for the party. They have masses of energy and will want to burn some of it off – so make sure that you have plenty of room and plan some well-organized activities.

7-year-olds: At this age, children can understand the rules of games and are quite co-operative, so they will enjoy some organized team games. Make sure that everyone has a chance to shine, or it may all end in tears.

8-year-olds: This is the age when many children prefer single-sex parties. Many of them also prefer to have an activity party such as swimming, ten-pin bowling or a visit to a puppet theatre. This can be quite expensive, so if you're paying to take them out, try to organize tea at home or a picnic to cut down the cost.

9-year-olds: Children can be quite difficult at this age because they are becoming competitive and tend to show off. Team games are excellent, as is anything that gives them a platform to perform – say, a quiz or charades, or even something more physical like a football match or sports party.

10-year-olds: Double figures mean a leap into maturity, and ten-year-olds will want the party to be as much of a success as you do. They will help you choose the appropriate games and organize the whole event.

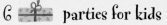

Invitations

Get your party off to a flying start with these jazzy invitation ideas.

Personalized invitations are terrific fun and these are simple to make. If you're having a themed party, set the scene right from the start with the party invitation.

Dangle planets and moons from black cotton for a 3-D space effect.

Curiosity will get the better of this cat – simply fold some card in half and cut the top of a cat's head out of the back of the card.

Get off your horse and make this Wild West-style invitation. Push a pencil through the card to make bullet holes, then rub the edges with black crayon.

Pumpkin and ghost paperchains make really fantastic invitations for a spooky party.

Get the party magic working early by sending invitations on silver wands.

Dangling snakes twist and twirl in a light breeze. Cut a serpent spiral out of coloured card and make a hole in the end to thread some string through.

Hints and tips

Keep your invitation design simple – you will need to draw it several times.

☆ **Pop-up invitations are fun to receive, and are surprisingly easy to make.**

☆ **Gold or silver pens are readily available at most stationers', and look very effective on dark cards.**

☆ **Snakes, pigs and sharks all make great invitations, or you could use the birthday child's favourite animal.**

X marks the spot: rub brown crayon along the torn edges of the card to make the map look older.

Flowery party pigs are a great motif for invitations. Wrap pink wool around a pipe cleaner to make a curly tail.

Everyone's a winner with these gold medal invitations – perfect for sports parties. Cut a small hole in the top so you can thread a ribbon through.

What to do

Clowning around

You will need:
★ **thin card**
★ **different-coloured paper or card**
★ **scissors**
★ **thin wire (fuse wire is ideal)**
★ **glue**

1 Cut a piece of card 30 x 15cm/12 x 6 inches. Fold in half. Open it out and make two 4cm/1½ inch cuts across fold. Push through central piece of card. Make a fold so it stands up. Decorate inside of card with coloured paper.

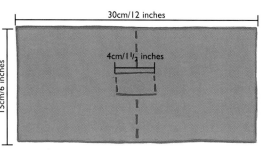

2 Cut a clown shape out of card. Your finished clown must not be taller than 13cm/5½ inches (including juggling balls). Bend thin wire above clown's head and stick to his back. Stick three card 'balls' on the wire.

3 Stick the clown to the small piece of card in the middle, and your jolly juggling clown is complete.

Pumpkin parade

You will need:
★ **thin orange card, about 60 x 13cm/24 x 5½ inches**
★ **yellow and orange paper**
★ **scissors or craft knife**
★ **glue**

1 Fold orange card in a zigzag into six sections. On the front, draw your pumpkin design making sure it goes right to the edges of the card. Using scissors or a craft knife, cut out shape, taking care not to cut the folded edges.

2 Open out your pumpkin paperchain, and decorate with the yellow and orange paper. Fold the card up again and cut out a mouth and eyes.

Shark shocker

You will need:

★ blue, white and grey card

★ scissors

★ glue

1 Fold a piece of grey card in half and draw a shark outline on it. Allow about 1cm/ 1/2 inch at the bottom for the tabs. Add eyes, gills and teeth.

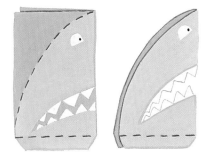

2 Fold a piece of blue card in half. Cut out a big water splash and several drops from the white card. Stick these on blue card. Glue along the tabs.

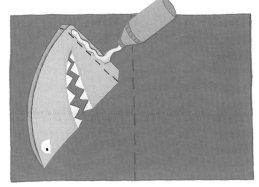

3 Position the shark in the middle of the water splash and at an angle to the centre fold. Close the card and allow the glue to dry.

Dinosaur badge card

You will need:

★ thin card

★ different-coloured paper or card

★ scissors

★ glue

★ thin elastic

★ safety pin and sticky tape

1 Fold a piece of card in half. Stick on coloured paper bushes and sand. Make two small holes in the middle and thread through a small piece of elastic. Tie the ends at the back.

2 Cut out a dinosaur shape. Attach a safety pin to the dinosaur with sticky tape, then pin it through the loop of elastic on front of card.

Possible venues

If the thought of hordes of overexcited kids tearing around your home fills you with dread, the answer might be to hold the party somewhere else.

If you decide to hold the party away from home, there are a few things you should take into account. If you are going any distance, you need to recruit the services (and cars!) of some of the other parents to help you with transport. Where young children are concerned, there should always be at least one adult for every three children, to help with supervision – toilet trips, organizing the refreshments, or just to offer a cuddle when necessary.

Ideas away from home

Here are some ideas for venues and parties that you can hold away from home.

Swimming pool parties: Check with your local swimming pool whether – and when – you can hold a party there. Find out if they provide a lifeguard, and if not, make sure you have enough adults coming to help you supervise the children. Try to keep all the games in the water. Children running around the outside of the pool is a recipe for disaster. Don't forget that the children are bound to have different swimming abilities, and ensure that there are some games for the less

competent – perhaps involving swimming aids such as arm bands or rubber rings – as well as the good swimmers. Some swimming pools have a special room where the children can eat their tea, and some actually provide the food. You will have to bring the cake.

Ice skating parties: Check with your local skating rink whether it is possible to hold a party there. Ask if they provide instructors, who will teach the children the rudiments of skating and make sure that they are safe on the ice. If not, ensure that there will be enough adults to supervise the children. Some skating rinks have a special room where the children can hold the party and eat their tea after skating, and some provide the food. As with swimming parties, though, you will have to bring the cake.

Theatre parties: Some children's theatres and puppet theatres are geared up for parties. The children watch the play and then they can go to a special section of the theatre café to eat their tea. Sometimes you have to prepare and bring this yourself, or sometimes they will provide it. Either way, you will have to bring the cake.

Beach parties: If you live near the sea, a nice idea is to go to the beach, where you can organize lots of activities on the shore – building sand castles, making sculptures or building models out of driftwood, collecting shells, and even digging for mussels or clams.

Make sure that there are enough adults to supervise the children, and don't allow them to venture off on their own.

Parties in the park: Take the children to your local park and organize plenty of different sporty games as well as some silly ones (see page 68), and create your very own Park Olympiad. Have lots of prizes and try to ensure that everyone wins something.

If the weather is very hot, take plenty of drinks, ask the children to bring sunhats (have a few to spare just in case), supply sun cream, and try to base yourself somewhere where there is some shade.

It may be fun to have a picnic, but make sure that most of the Olympiad events take place before eating. If you've planned an outdoor party, it's always sensible to have a contingency plan to fall back on in case it pours with rain and the whole event is a wash-out! Check what's on at the local cinema or hire a video just in case.

Other party ideas

There are plenty of other parties you can hold, depending on your local facilities and what your child is interested in. Consider the following:

★ an arty-crafty party, perhaps involving a competition
★ a cooking party
★ a junior disco
★ a cook-out and sleep-out-in-the-garden party
★ tennis with coaching games
★ five- and ten-pin bowling
★ soft indoor gymnasium for your children

★ trampolining (this needs close supervision)
★ waterslide park for older children
★ rollerblading (in-line skating)
★ junior racing car tracks
★ horse riding – your local stables might let you hold a mini-gymkhana
★ softball or football games
★ cricket match or sevens
★ pitch and putt
★ being part of an audience at a TV show

Places of interest to visit

The idea is that the place will entertain the children rather than you having to provide the entertainment. Places that make good party venues for a group of children include:

★ science museum – some museums even allow the children to have a sleep over
★ football/sports stadium
★ adventure playground
★ theme park
★ farm or zoo
★ toy museum
★ car museum
★ circus
★ sports match
★ aquarium
★ theatre
★ concert
★ ballet

After a couple of hours or so, you will need to feed the kids, so make sure that there is a restaurant or picnic area and toilet facilities nearby.

Entertainers

Many parents can't face the prospect of entertaining a group of demanding kids for two hours. That's why professional entertainers have become so popular.

Entertainers don't come cheap but they can be invaluable for children over the age of three or four. If you choose the right one, you are guaranteed a successful party.

Finding an entertainer

The best way of finding an entertainer is by word of mouth – preferably from another parent who has recently thrown a successful party. But this is not always possible.

Other ways are to look at advertisements in your local newspaper or telephone directory, but this is probably the least reliable method of all because there's no way of knowing how good someone is. If you call up someone cold, ask for a recommendation from someone for whom they have worked recently. If the entertainers operate under a character name, such as 'Tommy the Clown' or 'Twinkle Toes', they may be part of an organization that uses many different people dressed up as the same character and some may be better than others. It is therefore well worth finding out who is the best and making sure you get that one.

Asking the right questions

Different entertainers provide different services, and it is always advisable to check exactly what they will provide for the money.

★ **Do they just provide the entertainment, or do they also organize games?**
★ **Is their show suitable for your child's age?**
★ **Do they give prizes? If so, what sort and how many? Will every child receive one?**
★ **Do they give going-home presents?**
★ **Do they help with the tea?**
★ **How long do they stay?**
★ **Do they have a helper?**

Which entertainer?

There is a whole host of entertainers to choose from. You know your child and will be aware of what would suit him or her. Your best bet is probably to choose an entertainer who doesn't concentrate too much on any one thing, as the children might get bored.

Magicians: They will provide a show of magic tricks. Many of them make balloon sculptures for the children to take away – make sure that they make one for each child – and the highlight may be a live rabbit which all the children can pet.

Sports organizers: Many sports clubs have qualified instructors who will organize a children's sports party. There are as many different types of sports party as there are sports, such as football, tennis, swimming, baseball and gymnastics.

Clowns: These come in many guises but most of them just make the children laugh. Some of them perform magic tricks and others also organize games.

Face painters: This is a very popular form of entertainment. Imagine being able to transform yourself into a monster, a cat or an alien. The only drawback is that each child has to wait for their turn.

Puppeteers: These come in all shapes and sizes, from traditional hand puppets to beach booth characters. A clever puppeteer will involve the children in the show but you cannot expect the children to sit still for too long, so ask if they organize games as well.

Jugglers: A juggler will not keep the attention of children for very long unless he is also teaching them the skill. This is most suitable for older children and the juggler can also organize some games.

Craft projects: There are many enthusiastic arts and crafts teachers who enjoy spending an hour or two over the weekend taking a group project. Make sure each child takes something home.

Storytellers: These appeal to more imaginative children. Storytelling parties work best for a maximum of eight children.

Dance teachers: If your child is mad about dance, a dance party is just the thing. Ask your local dance school if they have a teacher who will organize a party.

Animal trainers: They will bring a collection of animals to the party and introduce them to the children. Some have cats, rabbits, guinea pigs and so on, while some have more exotic animals such as tarantulas and snakes.

Advance booking

Good entertainers need to be booked in advance, so ring as soon as possible. Write to them to confirm exactly what they have agreed to provide, and include the following information:

★ **the date and time of the party**
★ **the age of the child**
★ **the number of children**
★ **the address of the party**
★ **how long the party will be**

Ring a few days later to check that they have received the details. Ring again, two or three days before the party, to make sure that the entertainer is definitely going to turn up. This sounds laborious but it is well worth it.

It is advisable to have a contingency plan ready even if you do hire an entertainer, as they may have a sudden illness or some problem that causes them to cancel. Be prepared and check out the local cinema in advance or hire a video, or have that old standby 'pass-the-parcel' ready – just in case of disaster.

Setting the scene

Parties are all about celebration, which is why it is so important to set the scene. This instantly says 'party' and gets everyone in the mood right from the word go.

There are several ways of setting the scene, the most important one being decorations. These can either be bought ready-made or, if you're feeling creative, they can be homemade.

Buying decorations

There are lots of decorations on the market that can create an instant party atmosphere. These include balloons, streamers, banners, themed paper tablecloths, paper plates and cups, spray streamers, party hats, horns, and so on.

The best place to get these is one of the many specialist party shops around, which are now becoming increasingly common. They are well worth a visit anyway, if only to get some inspirational ideas.

If you don't have a specialist party shop near you, many of these items can be bought at a local toy shop or stationer's. The streamers and banners can be kept in a special box and used each time you have a party.

Balloons can be blown up simply with puff, but you can also buy special hand-held pumps. These are inexpensive and easy to use – even by the children themselves. Some party shops have heavy-duty pumps, which are even easier and more efficient to use, and they may hire you one for a nominal charge if you buy your balloons from them.

Most party shops will fill balloons with helium for you. If you are using the balloons outside, however, be sure to secure them firmly, as otherwise – given half a chance – they will just float away, never to be seen again.

However you've filled them, balloons should then be grouped in bunches and tied. It's a good idea to tie them to the front door or the garden gate to announce the party zone to visitors.

Many people hold their parties in a village, school

Can I help?

Kids enjoy all the party preparations, such as blowing up balloons.

or church hall. In this way, they don't have to worry about the mess, the noise or the space. But these places usually need cheering up with some decorations, so take some with you and dress up the space a few hours before the party begins.

Homemade decorations

Your child will greatly appreciate it if you make some of the decorations for the party yourself, and proud cries of 'Mummy made those' will be heard repeatedly. This may be the first party you've given for your child, but it certainly won't be the last (not if it's the wild success that it's bound to be!).

There are lots of useful items for making your own decorations, which you can keep at the ready in a box for when the occasion demands.
Useful things to have available include:

- ★ corrugated cardboard
- ★ cardboard boxes
- ★ old newspapers
- ★ old sheets/fabric remnants
- ★ coloured string

- ★ ribbons
- ★ tinsel
- ★ paints
- ★ magic markers
- ★ glue and glitter glue
- ★ sticky tape
- ★ scissors

Things to make

It may be worth investing some time making a few decorations that you can use again and again. If you're giving a birthday party, for example, you can make a birthday banner with the child's name and age, or just 'Happy Birthday', then it can be used for anyone in the family. A Mexican piñata (see page 75) is a great idea. It provides a wonderful climax to the party and will be a talking point at parties for years to come.

Music

Lastly, don't forget that music is important in making any party go with a swing. Each age group has their favourite tunes, from nursery rhymes for the very young to the latest hit records for older children. A portable CD player will come in handy, and you can always put on your favourite music while you are preparing for the party just to get you in the mood.

Themed parties

If you're stuck for ideas, a themed party may be the answer. It's not only great fun, it also gives you a framework within which to plan those all-important details – the costumes, the food, even the games.

If this is the first themed party that you've given for your child, it may be worth spending some time making the fancy dress costumes yourself from bits and bobs in your store cupboard. You will be able to use them again and again for future parties. There are a lot of things you probably have already around the house that will come in useful for costume making and dressing up. These include the following:

- ★ leotards
- ★ leggings
- ★ T-shirts, long- and short-sleeved
- ★ polo-neck sweaters and T-shirts
- ★ kitchen paper rolls
- ★ corrugated cardboard
- ★ garbage bags
- ★ bubble wrap
- ★ loo rolls
- ★ cotton wool
- ★ knitting wool
- ★ sticky-back Velcro
- ★ scraps of fabric
- ★ pieces of net
- ★ old sheets
- ★ old clothes
- ★ Wellington boots
- ★ tennis shoes
- ★ gym shoes
- ★ felt
- ★ old jeans
- ★ PVA adhesive
- ★ adhesive tape
- ★ double-sided sticky tape
- ★ glitter glue
- ★ orange net bags
- ★ tissue paper
- ★ adhesive for sticking felt
- ★ card

Making the costumes

Fancy dress costumes can be bought or hired from specialist party or costume shops, but that's an easy way out. If you have the time and energy, it is a lot more satisfying to make something yourself. Your child is bound to appreciate your efforts and, as a result, your child's costume will look completely different from everyone else's.

All the fancy dress costumes that we've created for this book look absolutely magnificent – we hope you agree. But

Measuring your child

This illustration shows you how to take your child's measurements.

across the chest and over the shoulder blades.

1 Height
Measure from top of the head to ground without shoes.

2 Chest
Place the tape measure round the body so it is positioned

3 Waist
Measure round the natural waistline.

4 Inside leg
Place the tape measure at the very top of the inside leg and measure to the required length.

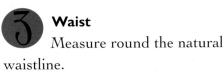

don't be put off – they're not difficult. They are all, in fact, surprisingly easy to make and require no special dressmaking skills or fancy equipment. The instructions are all straightforward and very simple to follow. You can use your own imagination and incorporate whatever fabrics and accessories that you have to hand in order to add your own special, personal touch.

All of the patterns that are given here should fit children between the ages of about five and nine. In the box above, we tell you how to measure your child to adapt the pattern to his or her age and size.

All the patterns are shown in miniature. To scale them up to the correct size, it is best to use squared paper and simply transfer the drawings, following the measurements that are indicated on all the pattern pieces.

The best clothes to wear under any dressing-up costumes are matching-colour T-shirts or polo necks, and leggings (tights will be too slippery unless the child also wears shoes).

Dinosaur party

Dinosaurs are a great favourite with all children. To create the right atmosphere, turn the room into a primeval rainforest with giant fronds and ferns.

This friendly dinosaur is not one of the man-eating species.

The hunter comes home after his hard day out in search of supper.

The well-dressed cavewoman keeps herself warm and snug in furs.

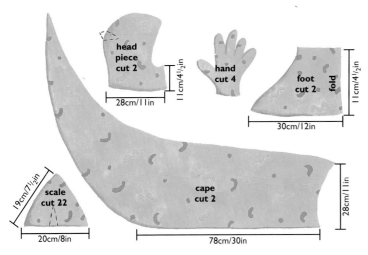

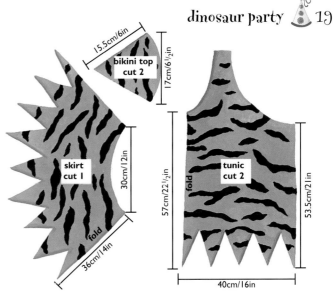

Dinosaur costume

You will need:

★ 1.5m/60 inches yellow felt, 1.5m/60 inches wide

★ sticky-back Velcro

★ orange, brown, purple and green
   fabric paints

1 Draw the pattern to scale and cut out the fabric. Draw round your child's hand and cut out. Paint each piece and leave to dry for at least three hours.

2 Sew all the darts on the head piece and on the scales.

3 Pin half the scales, right sides together, on to one side of the head and cape pieces. Make sure the scales are pointing downwards. Then pin on the other side of the head and cape pieces, right sides together (sandwiching the scales in between them). Sew together and turn to right side.

4 Gather the cape around the neck and sew to the head piece. Attach sticky-back Velcro to the neck to fasten. Sew the feet along the front seam. Sew around the outline of the hand pieces, and slip on like a glove.

Cave people's costumes

For each costume you will need:

★ 1m/40 inches animal-print fur fabric

★ elastic

★ black tape/ribbon

★ scraps of fur fabric for arm and leg bands

1 Cut out the fabric for the cave people's costumes, following the pattern.

2 Sew together the side and shoulders of the caveman's tunic.

3 Sew the side seam of the cavewoman's skirt. Then pin and sew a casing around the waist. Insert some elastic to fit the size of your child's waist and tie the ends together in a knot.

4 For the girl's bikini top, sew the two cups together in the middle, then attach tape to the cups to fit around the neck and around the back.

5 Cut the animal-print fur fabric scraps into 5cm/2 inch wide strips and use these to decorate the arms and legs, and to tie the hair.

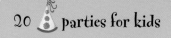
Princess party

Little girls are guaranteed to love these costumes so much that they'll use them again and again – not just for parties but for dressing-up games at home, too.

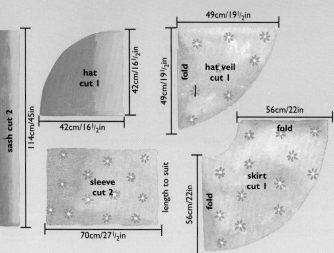

sash cut 2
114cm/45in

hat
cut 1
42cm/16½in
42cm/16½in

49cm/19½in
fold
hat veil
cut 1
49cm/19½in

56cm/22in
fold
skirt
cut 1
fold
56cm/22in

sleeve
cut 2
70cm/27½in
length to suit

For each costume

You will need:
★ 1 leotard
★ 2m/80 inches chiffon (or net curtaining),
    1.5m/60 inches wide
★ 1m/40 inches bias binding
★ elastic
★ gold or silver ribbon
★ card
★ glue
★ 1m/40 inches gold or silver fabric,
    1.2m/48 inches wide

1 Draw pattern to scale and cut out sleeves, hat veil and skirt (in a full circle). Hem with zigzag stitch. Sew casing around waist, leaving a gap. Cut elastic to fit waist, thread through and knot.

2 Zigzag stitch around the edge of the sleeves and gather around the top of them. Then pin the sleeves to the shoulders or sleeves of the leotard, and sew these in place.

3 Stitch the sash together with a centre seam. Then hem around the edges by hand.

4 Cut out hat from card and cover in fabric. Then glue together the back edges of the hat. Hem around the edges of the hat veil, and then sew to the top of the hat. Sew elastic to the hat to fit under the chin.

Princesses

Fairytales and films, between them, have encouraged lots of little girls to dream of being a beautiful fairy princess. This may not be the best preparation for real life, but indulge their dreams this once by letting them dress the part – they'll look terrific!

There's nothing that makes
a little girl feel more elegant
than a tall hat.

Outer space party

This is the ideal theme for a group of imaginative eight-year-old children. The birthday child can be made the captain of the spaceship, in charge of the control panel.

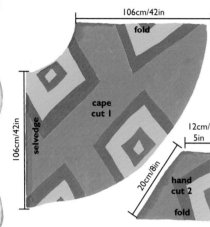

106cm/42in

fold

cape
cut 1

selvedge

106cm/42in

12cm/
5in

20cm/8in

hand
cut 2

fold

15cm/6in

10cm/4in

114cm/45in

belt
cut 1

fold

30cm/12in

30cm/12in

shoulder piece
cut 2

60cm/23½in

hat
cut 1

60cm/23½in

39cm/15½in

arm band
cut 2

42cm/16½in

leg
band
cut 2

to fit waist

belt
cut 1

Alien costume

You will need:
★ 1.2 x 2m/48 x 80 inches bubble wrap
★ acrylic paint for bubble wrap
★ acrylic spray paint for head piece
★ sticky-back Velcro
★ inexpensive plastic football for head piece
★ face paint

1 Draw the pattern to scale and cut out the bubble wrap for the cloak, gloves and belt. Decorate with paint and make a fastening around the neck with the sticky-back Velcro.

2 Cut the football in half, spray with paint and allow to dry. When you have applied face paint, put on the head piece.

Spaceman costume

You will need:
★ 4 large sheets of silver card
★ sticky-back Velcro
★ fluorescent tape, for decoration

1 Cut out all the shapes for the spaceman in silver card, following the pattern, and assemble the pieces using the Velcro.

2 Decorate this supersonic costume with well-positioned strips of fluorescent tape, as shown in the picture.

No space trip would be
complete without an
amazing alien.

Turtle-necks,
leggings and spray-
on glitter make these
out-of-this-world
costumes complete.

Spooky party

Kids just love dressing up as ghoulish ghosts.
To create the right atmosphere, spray cobwebs
on the windows and hang spiders from the ceiling.

Witch costume

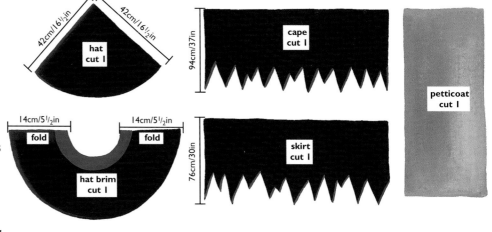

You will need:
★ **2m/80 inches net**
★ **elastic**
★ **2m/80 inches green ribbon**
★ **2 strong black plastic bin bags**
★ **2 pieces of black card**
★ **glitter paint**
★ **empty orange net bag**
★ **1 green plastic rubbish bin bag**

1 Cut out the net to twice the length of your child for the petticoat. Fold in half lengthwise and make a casing along the fold. Thread elastic through the casing and tie into a knot.

2 Open the top of the black plastic bag and pull into a cylinder shape to make a skirt. Snip the hem into random zigzags and cut holes 5cm/2 inches from the top and 7cm/3 inches apart. Thread the ribbon through the holes. For the cape: cut along top and sides of the second bag, and open it out flat. Cut holes about 5cm/2 inches from the top and 7cm/3 inches apart. Thread through the ribbon and tie into a cape.

3 Cut out hat and brim from card and decorate. Glue back edges of hat together

and attach brim, snipping inside sections at intervals. For wig: cut green bag into 2.5cm/1 inch strips and pull a strip through each hole in the net bag, securing with a knot in the middle. Thread elastic through the outer holes in the net bag and knot in the middle.

Ghost

You will need:
★ **1 old sheet**
★ **2 scraps of black felt, cut into 8cm/3$\frac{1}{2}$ inch circles**
★ **glue**

1 Place the sheet over your child's head and mark the position of the eyes on the outside of it.

2 Glue the black felt circles in place, then cut out the centres, making two peep holes.

Mummy

You will need:
- ★ 3 white toilet rolls
- ★ masking tape

Wrap the child loosely in white toilet paper. Before you start winding it around them, make sure their limbs are slightly bent or they will find it difficult to walk. Secure the paper with masking tape.

Few people would like to meet this witch on a dark night!

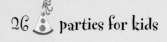

Underwater party

Transform the room into a giant aquarium with tinsel, streamers, strips of cellophane and shells. Hang tropical fish and jellyfish from the ceiling.

Every little girl will jump at the chance of being a mermaid – with legs!

A scuba diver wears black, a swimming mask, snorkel and flippers. Make an aqualung with two washing-up bottles sprayed blue.

The King of the Sea looks suitably venerable!

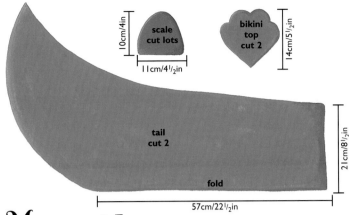

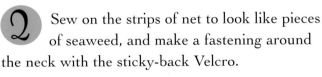

Mermaid

You will need:

- ★ 1m/40 inches green felt, 1.5m/60in wide
- ★ 25cm/10 inches of felt in each of three colours for scales
- ★ 2m/80 inches gold braid to

assemble bikini
- ★ glue
- ★ gold glitter glue
- ★ 2 plastic bags
- ★ empty orange net bag, for wig
- ★ elastic

1 Draw pattern and cut out tail, bikini top, and as many scales as you want. Glue scales on to tail, starting from the bottom and grading colours as you go. Keep some scales to cover the side seams.

2 Sew the side seams of the tail, leaving an opening for the casing. Make the waist casing and thread through elastic to fit your child's waist. Knot the ends.

3 Sew a double seam to reinforce tail, and glue on the remaining scales to cover side seams. Decorate tail with glitter glue. Make the top as for cavewoman on page 19. Decorate with glitter glue.

4 To make wig, cut plastic bags into 2.5cm/ 1 inch strips. Thread elastic through holes in net bag. Pull through plastic strips and knot in centre.

Neptune

You will need:

- ★ 2m/80 inches dark green lining fabric, wide enough to fit child's height from shoulder to floor
- ★ 1m/40 inches each green, turquoise and yellow net
- ★ sticky-back Velcro

- ★ gold card
- ★ stapler
- ★ 1m/40 inches gold braid
- ★ 2 white plastic bags
- ★ empty orange net bag, for wig
- ★ elastic
- ★ beard

1 Draw the pattern to scale and cut out the cape and the strips of green, turquoise and yellow net. Hem the front edges of the cape and around the bottom edge, and gather neck.

2 Sew on the strips of net to look like pieces of seaweed, and make a fastening around the neck with the sticky-back Velcro.

3 Cut out Neptune's crown, following the pattern. Staple the back together to fit your child's head.

4 Make the wig using the white plastic bags and following the instructions for the mermaid's wig, left.

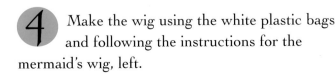

Wild West party

This is the perfect theme for boisterous boys aged about eight or nine, who are bound to enjoy dressing up as rough and rugged cowboys.

This is the age at which children enjoy a sleep over. Don't invite too many kids or they'll never get any sleep!

Sleeping over

Six is a sensible maximum for a sleep over party – more than that and they won't sleep. Invite them with their sleeping bags and preferably not before about 4 or 5pm. Summer is the best time of year for this sort of theme, as you can combine it with a barbecue, after some games. A cowboy video is a good way for the children to wind down before they go to bed.

Dressing up as cowboys (and cowgirls) is easy.

Cowboy hats and sheriff badges complete the picture.

Cowboys

Cowboys do not need any special outfits, and this is therefore one of the easiest fancy dress costumes of all, requiring absolutely minimal work – just a little (inexpensive) shopping. All young cowboys need is some jeans, a checked shirt, a bandana (scarf) and some artificial stubble with face paint. Cowboy hats are easily available from fancy dress and party shops.

Playing with the cowboys

A good game to play at a Wild West party is a scavenger hunt. Play it in pairs or small groups, each of which is given a bag to carry their booty. For older children, give them a list of things to find and tell them the limits of the area for their search. Give them a time limit to find the objects and blow a whistle or ring a bell when time is up. Some ideas might include:

★ a dropped sweet wrapper
★ a forked twig
★ 3 white stones
★ 5 blades of grass
★ a feather
★ a dandelion
★ a leaf

Face painting

Dressing up as cowboys is a good opportunity for some imaginative face painting, with moustaches, beards, scars and stubble being firm favourites.

Clown party

A clown party is a great theme for young children between the ages of four and seven. Hire a clown entertainer or some face paint artists.

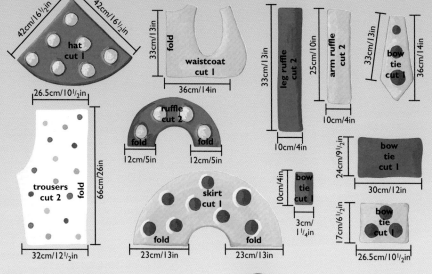

Boy clown

You will need:

★ 1m/40 inches trouser fabric, 1.5m/60 inches wide

★ 1m/40 inches felt, 1.5m/60 inches wide for the waistcoat, bow tie and ruffles

★ 30 x 30cm/12 x 12 inches red felt for spots on bow tie

★ 2 large buttons

★ 1m/40 inches red ric-rac

★ elastic

★ 2 pompoms made from rainbow-coloured wool

★ sticky-back Velcro

1 Draw pattern to scale and cut out all the pieces. With right sides facing, sew the trousers around the crutch and along the inside legs. Make a casing around the waist and ankles, and thread with elastic. Sew on trimming for waistcoat, stitch up shoulder seams and sew on two giant buttons.

2 Decorate yellow bow tie with red spots. Thread both bows through the blue casing, oversew in place and stitch on yellow tie. Sew bias binding as a casing in the centre of ruffles, thread with elastic and tie off.

Girl clown

You will need:
★ 1m/40 inches felt,
    1.5m/60 inches wide for skirt
★ 75cm/30 inches felt for ruffles
★ scraps of felt for spots
★ 1m/40 inches yellow net, for petticoat
★ 3m/120 inches elastic
★ 1.5m/60 inches yellow bias binding
★ 1 pompom made from rainbow-coloured wool
★ glue

1 Draw pattern to scale and cut out the skirt, petticoat, ruffles and spots (using scraps).

2 Make skirt and neck ruffle by sewing a casing. Insert elastic and tie off. Decorate with coloured spots.

3 Make petticoat by sewing a casing along fold and inserting elastic. Sew ends together.

4 Make leg/hand ruffles by sewing bias binding and inserting elastic. Sew pompom on T-shirt.

Clowning around comes naturally to most kids.

Clown hats

You will need:
★ 1 sheet of card
★ 50cm/20 inches each yellow and blue felt
★ scraps of red felt
★ glue
★ 1 ball of rainbow-coloured wool for the hair
★ 2 pompoms made from rainbow-coloured wool

1 Cut out the hats from card, following the pattern, and cover with felt. Then cut out 40cm/16 inch lengths of wool in bundles of eight. Sew to edge of hat and trim.

2 Sew pompom to hat and decorate with spots. Staple edges of hat to form a cone.

Attach Velcro to back of pompoms and stick on top of the shoes.

Pirate party

Hoist the sails and pull up the gangplank – this is strictly for intrepid children, as these fearless pirates venture into murky, shark-infested waters.

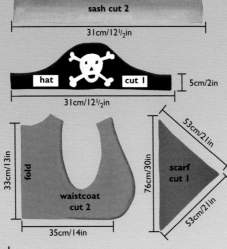

26.5cm/10½in

sash cut 2
31cm/12½in

hat   cut 1
31cm/12½in
5cm/2in

trousers cut 2
fold
66cm/26½in
31cm/12½in

waistcoat cut 2
fold
33cm/13in
35cm/14in

scarf cut 1
53cm/21in
76cm/30in
53cm/21in

Shiver me timbers! Pirates rule the sea at partytime.

Pirate costume

You will need:

★ 1m/40 inches cotton fabric, 1.2m/48 inches wide, for trousers
★ 1m/40 inches felt, 1.5m/60 inches wide, for waistcoat
★ 1.5m/60 inches braid
★ 4 buttons
★ 75cm/30 inches cotton fabric, for sash and scarf
★ black and white card
★ glue
★ elastic
★ silver card for buckles
★ sticky-back Velcro

1 Draw pattern to scale, cut out pieces, and make trousers following clown instructions on page 30.

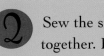

2 Sew the shoulder seams of the waistcoat together. Hand stitch the braid around the edge and sew on the buttons.

3 Hem the edges of both the scarf and the sash. Cut out the hat from the black card, then trace off the skull and crossbones and cut out of white card and glue on. Measure your child's head and attach sticky-back Velcro to fasten the hat at the back.

4 Make buckles out of silver card and attach them to shoes with the Velcro.

Scallywag costume

You will need:
★ 1m/40 inches felt, 1.5m/60 inches wide
★ elastic

1 Draw the pattern to scale and cut out the trousers. Cut zigzags around the bottoms of both trouser legs.

2 Sew around crutch and inside legs. Then make a casing around the waist and thread through the elastic. Make hat, sash, scarf and shoe buckles as for the pirate.

Land ahoy!

Skull and crossbones, eye patches, moustaches and blacked-out teeth... all designed to make these nice little boys look as fierce as can be!

Aargh, Jim lad... me hearties!

Sandwiches

Above all, celebration sandwiches should be special. They can be made from different sorts of bread, and filled with a variety of fillings – both sweet and savoury as the mood takes you.

Sandwich secrets

☆ **Make sandwiches with bread that is one day old, as it will be firmer.**

☆ **Chill a sandwich loaf before you slice it.**

☆ **A hot knife makes it easier to cut bread.**

☆ **Keep sandwiches fresh by placing them in plastic bags or covering them with a clean, damp cloth.**

☆ **Take margarine or butter out of the fridge to soften a couple of hours before you begin.**

☆ **Use different types of bread to add variety to your party sandwiches. Choose from rye, granary, baguette or French stick, ciabatta, chollah, pitta, rolls or baps and muffins.**

Pinwheels

Makes 36–42
You will need:

★ **I long uncut brown or white sandwich loaf**

★ **butter or margarine, softened**

★ **chosen filling – sweet or savoury**

Cut bread into thin slices lengthways and remove the crusts. Spread with butter or margarine and then add the filling. Roll up each slice of bread and secure with foil or cling film. Chill for an hour before cutting into slices.

Smooth fillings, such as jam or peanut butter, will get you in a whirl.

Chocolate bagels

Serves 5
You will need:
★ **5 bagels**
★ **250g/8oz melted chocolate**
★ **slices of fruit, such as banana, strawberry and pineapple**

Slice the bagels in half and remove all the doughy white inside from the bottom halves. Fill with melted chocolate and add the fruit before it sets. Add the top half and heat in the oven until the bagels are crisp.

Warn the children to take care when they bite into the bagels as the melted chocolate will be hot.

Egg mayonnaise

Makes 4–5 sandwiches
You will need:
★ **4 hard-boiled eggs**
★ **1 teaspoon butter**
★ **2 tablespoons mayonnaise**
★ **salt and pepper**

Rinse the hot hard-boiled eggs under cold water to prevent the yolks turning black. Shell and chop or mash the eggs with a fork. Add the butter and mayonnaise and mix well. Season to taste.

Slices of celery, green, yellow and red peppers, sweet cherry tomatoes and savoury sticks make delicious edible cargo.

If you have problems balancing the sandwiches on the cocktail sticks, put them on a piece of card.

Add the finishing touch to the train by cutting a wisp of smoke from an extra slice of white bread.

Eggspress train

Allow 1–2 sandwiches per child
You will need:
★ **brown and white sliced bread**
★ **butter or margarine, softened**
★ **egg mayonnaise filling**
★ **other savoury fillings**
★ **carrots, celery, peppers, tomatoes and savoury sticks**

Butter the bread and sandwich together with fillings of your choice. Cut into carriage-shaped rectangles and make an engine. Push slices of carrot on to cocktail sticks for wheels. Balance the sandwiches on the sticks and decorate the tops.

Rude rolls

Makes 10 rolls
You will need:

★ 10 different-shaped bread rolls
★ butter or margarine, softened
★ ham, sausage, salami and cheese for fillings
★ salad ingredients for decoration
★ wooden cocktail sticks

Cut each roll halfway across to make a mouth and spread the inside with butter or margarine. Cut the meat into tongue shapes and the cheese into teeth shapes.

Arrange the meat and cheese inside the rolls. Decorate with eyes, noses, ears and hair, securing them with the cocktail sticks (remember to remove these before eating!).

Carrot sticks will make your hair stand on end!

Open sandwiches

Makes 4 sandwiches
You will need:

★ 4 slices of brown or white bread
★ various toppings, such as cream and cottage cheese, lemon curd, chocolate spread, fruit, vegetables, salami, eggs, cress, sprinkles and sweets

Spread a sweet or savoury topping on each slice of bread. Decorate the topping, sweet on sweet, savoury on savoury, making faces, boats or flowers.

Get fruity with chocolate spread.

Radishes and olives make eyes at you.

Sail away on a sea of cottage cheese in a cucumber boat.

Can I help?

Encourage your child's creativity by getting her to design the pictures for the sandwiches.

Dips & other savouries

The secret to successful savoury food at parties is to have a variety of colourful snacks that look as appealing as the sweet treats.

Things to dip

Carrots, celery, cucumber, mushrooms, cauliflower florets, cherry tomatoes, radishes, crisps and toast.

Spinach dip

Serves 8
You will need:
★ 175g/6oz frozen spinach, defrosted
★ 150g/5oz soured cream
★ 2 tablespoons mayonnaise
★ salt and pepper

Strain the spinach in a sieve and pat dry with kitchen paper. Put all the ingredients in a food processor and blend together.

Cream cheese dip

Serves 8
You will need:
★ 250g/8oz cream cheese
★ 150g/5 oz soured cream
★ 2 tablespoons chopped chives
★ salt and pepper

Put all the ingredients in a food processor and blend together.

Cheesy biscuits

Makes about 25 biscuits
You will need:
★ 125g/4oz margarine
★ 250g/8oz plain flour
★ pinch of salt
★ 2 egg yolks
★ 50g/2oz grated Cheddar cheese
★ 2 tablespoons tomato ketchup
★ 1 egg, beaten

Preheat the oven to 200°C/400°F/ Gas Mark 6. Rub the margarine, flour and salt together in a bowl until it resembles breadcrumbs. Stir in the egg yolks, grated cheese and tomato ketchup. Mix together and form into a ball. Roll out the dough on a floured surface until it is about 5mm/ 1/4 inch thick, and cut into shapes. Transfer these to a greased baking tray and brush the tops with the beaten egg. Bake for 12 minutes and then transfer to a wire rack to cool.

Cheese dinosaur

Serves 8–10
You will need:
★ 1 pineapple
★ 1 kiwi fruit
★ 2 raisins
★ 250g/8oz hard cheese,
   such as Edam, Gouda or Cheddar

Cut a large slice from the top of the pineapple and remove some of the leaves. Cut the legs shape from the bottom of the fruit and scoop out the flesh (set aside to use later). Cut the cheese into triangles of various sizes. Cut the pineapple flesh into 1 cm/ ¹/₂ inch cubes. Insert cocktail sticks into the outside of the dinosaur and use them to secure first the pineapple pieces, then the cheese triangles. To make the head, peel the kiwi fruit and cut out a slit for the mouth. Attach the raisin eyes with cocktail sticks and use a pineapple leaf as the tongue. Attach the head to the body by pushing another cocktail stick through the centre of the crown of the pineapple.

Tomato and tuna owlets

Makes 12 owlets
You will need:
★ 12 small tomatoes
★ small can of tuna fish in brine, drained
★ 1 hard-boiled egg
★ 2 tablespoons mayonnaise
★ 2 teaspoons tomato ketchup
★ several stuffed green olives, cut into slices
★ lettuce, to serve

Halve the tomatoes and scoop out the seeds. Using a fork, mash together the tuna fish, egg, mayonnaise and tomato ketchup in a bowl. Pile the mixture into half of the cut tomatoes. Cut any remaining tomato halves into triangles for the beaks and ears. Decorate the filled tomato halves with the beaks and ears, then add the olive eyes. Serve on a nest of roughly torn lettuce.

Pizza & pasta

You simply can't beat pasta and pizza – both tasty and filling – when it comes to feeding a crowd of hungry kids.

Pizza dough

Makes two 20cm/8 inch pizzas
You will need:
★ 300g/10oz plain flour
★ 1 teaspoon salt
★ 15g/1 sachet dried yeast
★ 2 tablespoons olive oil
★ 250ml/8 fl oz hot water

Tomato sauce

Makes two 20cm/8 inch pizzas
You will need:
★ 2 tablespoons olive oil
★ 1 small onion, chopped
★ 2 tablespoons tomato purée
★ 1 x 400g/14oz can chopped tomatoes, drained
★ 1 teaspoon dried oregano
★ 1/2 teaspoon salt
★ 1/2 teaspoon sugar
★ pinch of ground black pepper

Heat the oil in a saucepan, add the chopped onion and cook gently for 5 minutes. Add the tomato purée, chopped tomatoes

Sift together the flour and salt, then add the yeast, oil and hot water, and mix into a dough. On a floured work surface, knead the dough for 5 minutes until it is shiny and elastic. Put the dough in a clean bowl, then cover, and leave to rise in a warm place for 1 hour.

and oregano, and season well. Cook for 15 minutes further, stirring occasionally. Allow to cool before spreading the sauce on the pizza base.

Pizza snake

Serves 8–10 children
You will need:
★ flour for rolling out dough
★ 2 tablespoons olive oil
★ 1 quantity of pizza dough
★ 1 quantity of tomato sauce
★ mozzarella cheese, sliced
★ 2 mushrooms, sliced
★ black olives
★ green pepper, for tongue

Preheat the oven to 180°C/350°F/Gas Mark 4. Roll the pizza dough into a sausage shape. Lay it in a spiral on a lightly oiled baking sheet and flatten to form the snake's body. Spread with tomato sauce, then add a row of mozzarella. Decorate the cheese with mushrooms and olives. Brush with olive oil and bake in the top of the oven for 15–20 minutes. Add small olive slices for the eyes and make a tongue with the green pepper.

Add a pair of beady eyes with black olives, and a hissing tongue with green pepper.

D-I-Y pizzas

If you don't have time to make your own pizza dough, buy ready-made bases and create your own designs.

Heavenly pizzas

Makes 2 mini pizzas
You will need:
★ I tablespoon olive oil
★ 2 small pizza bases
★ I quantity tomato sauce
★ 2 cheese slices
★ 3 thick mozzarella slices
To decorate:
★ black and green olives
★ slices of red pepper

Heat the oven to 190°C/375°F/ Gas Mark 5 and brush a baking sheet with oil. Cut out a star shape from one of the bases, using kitchen scissors. Cut out star shapes from the cheese slices and the rocket designs from the mozzarella cheese. Brush both pizza bases with oil and cover with tomato sauce. Bake for 8 minutes. Remove from the oven and cover the star pizza with the cheese slice stars and the round pizza with the rocket and star shapes. Decorate with olives, then bake for another 5 minutes.

Pizza tiger

Serves 4–6
You will need:
★ I tablespoon olive oil
★ 2 medium pizza bases
★ I quantity of tomato sauce
★ 250g/8oz Red Leicester cheese
★ 250g/8oz mozzarella cheese
★ 2 stuffed green olives, for eyes
★ fresh chives, for whiskers

Heat the oven to 190°C/375°F/ Gas Mark 5. Brush a large baking sheet with oil. Cut a tiger's head and tail from one of the bases, and a small piece from the top of the other base, where the head will fit. Assemble the tiger on the baking tray, brush with oil and cover with tomato sauce. Make the nose, ears and stripes out of cheese. Cook for 15–20 minutes, then remove from the oven and add the olive eyes and chive whiskers.

Tomato sauce for pasta

Serves 4–6
You will need:
* ★ 2 tablespoons olive oil
* ★ I large onion, peeled and finely chopped
* ★ 2 garlic cloves, crushed
* ★ 2 x 400g (14oz) cans chopped tomatoes
* ★ 2 tablespoons tomato purée
* ★ I teaspoon dried oregano
* ★ I teaspoon sugar
* ★ ½ teaspoon salt
* ★ freshly ground black pepper

Heat the oil in a saucepan, add the onion and garlic, and cook over medium heat for 5 minutes. Stir in the chopped tomatoes, tomato purée, oregano, sugar, salt and black pepper. Bring to the boil. Lower the heat and simmer for about 15 minutes, stirring from time to time. Serve with pasta.

Spaghetti bolognese

Serves 4–6
You will need:
* ★ 2 tablespoons oil
* ★ I onion, finely chopped
* ★ I garlic clove
* ★ 500g/I lb lean minced beef
* ★ 400g/14oz tomatoes, fresh or canned
* ★ I teaspoon dried basil
* ★ I bay leaf
* ★ I tablespoon Worcestershire sauce
* ★ ½ teaspoon salt
* ★ freshly ground black pepper
* ★ 300ml/½ pint water
* ★ beef stock cube
* ★ grated Parmesan, to serve

Heat the oil in a saucepan, add the onion and garlic, and cook over medium heat for 5 minutes. Brown the mince, stirring constantly. Add the chopped tomatoes, basil, bay leaf, Worcestershire sauce, salt, pepper and water, and sprinkle in the stock cube. Bring to the boil, reduce the heat to low, cover and simmer for 20 minutes. Remove the bay leaf and serve with grated Parmesan cheese.

Variations

Other easy pasta toppings include any of the following:
* ☆ olive oil and chopped fresh basil leaves
* ☆ butter
* ☆ any grated cheese
* ☆ pesto
* ☆ tuna fish
* ☆ chopped fresh tomatoes

If you don't eat beef, you can use minced lamb and a chicken stock cube instead.

B-B-Q news

Rain, rain go away – and let's have a barbecue. Kids always think it's a lot of fun eating outdoors – and it doesn't matter how much mess they make.

Mini-chicken satay

Makes 8–10 skewers
You will need:
★ **3 skinless chicken breast fillets**
For the marinade:
★ **4 tablespoons soy sauce**
★ **1 teaspoon sesame oil**
★ **1 tablespoon honey**
★ **1 tablespoon sherry or rice wine**
For the satay sauce:
★ **6 tablespoons peanut butter**
★ **1 clove garlic, crushed**
★ **1 tablespoon soy sauce**
★ **$1/2$ teaspoon chilli oil**
★ **4 tablespoons water**
★ **1 tablespoon rice vinegar**
★ **wooden skewers, soaked in water to prevent them burning**

Cut the chicken flesh into 1cm/$1/2$ inch cubes and thread about 10 on to each skewer. Make the marinade by combining all the ingredients. Pour over the skewered chicken and set aside for 1 hour. Barbecue the chicken for about 10 minutes, turning frequently. Meanwhile, make the satay sauce. Put all the ingredients into a food processor and blend until smooth. Serve the chicken skewers with the sauce.

Branded potatoes

Brand spuds with the initials of the guests or the age of the birthday child. Draw on your design with the point of a small knife, then carve out the skin and bake the potato in the oven or wrapped in foil in the coals.

Cut the corn cobs into pieces to make them easier to eat.

Corn on the cob

You will need:
- ★ I ear of corn per person
- ★ butter, to serve
- ★ salt and pepper

Husk the corn, making sure to remove all the silky threads. Dip it into cold water then wrap it tightly in kitchen foil. Grill on the barbecue, turning it frequently for about 10 minutes. Serve with lashings of butter, salt and pepper.

Mini-burgers

Makes about 18 burgers
You will need:
- ★ 500g/1lb steak mince
- ★ salt and pepper
- ★ 18 mini-buns
- ★ lettuce leaves, to serve

Lightly season the meat and form it into small, round, meatball-sized balls. Then flatten them into patties. Cook them for about 3 minutes each side on the griddle (they will be too small for most grills). Serve in the mini-buns with a few lettuce leaves and offer a selection of relishes for the children to help themselves.

Arrange all the barbecued food on a big serving plate and allow people to help themselves.

Vegetable kebabs

Makes 6–8 kebabs
You will need:
- ★ 8 cherry tomatoes
- ★ 12 mushrooms
- ★ 2 courgettes, sliced
- ★ I red pepper, cubed
- ★ I onion, cut into quarters
- ★ 6–8 wooden skewers, soaked in water to prevent burning
For the barbecue sauce:
- ★ 4 tablespoons tomato ketchup
- ★ 2 tablespoons Worcestershire sauce
- ★ I ¹/₂ tablespoons honey
- ★ I teaspoon lemon juice
- ★ pinch of cayenne pepper

Mix all the barbecue sauce ingredients in a saucepan and cook over a low heat for about 5 minutes, stirring constantly. Remove from the heat and cool. Thread the vegetables on to the skewers, alternating the colours. Brush with the sauce and grill on the barbecue for 10 minutes.

Barbecue tools

- ☆ Water spray (to put out flaming fat)
- ☆ Tongs and spatula for turning
- ☆ Tea towel for wiping hands
- ☆ Serving plate for cooked food

Sweet endings

Most children have a sweet tooth and what better time to indulge this than at partytime, with these mouthwatering and unusual treats?

Meringue creepy crawlies

Makes about 15 creepy crawlies
You will need:
★ 4 egg whites
★ 250g/8oz caster sugar
★ selection of food colouring
★ sweets, to decorate

Heat the oven to 140°C/275°F/Gas Mark 1. Line baking sheets with non-stick baking paper. Beat the egg whites until stiff. Add the sugar and continue beating for about 10 minutes. Divide the mixture into bowls and add a few drops of colouring to each one. Pipe each colour separately on to the baking sheets in different shapes, such as ladybirds, caterpillars, spiders, mice and snails. Decorate with sweets. Bake for 2 hours, then leave to cool.

Coconut ice

Makes 625g/1¼lb
You will need:
★ 500g/1 lb granulated sugar
★ 150ml/¼ pint milk
★ 150g/5oz desiccated coconut
★ pink food colouring

Line a 20cm/8 inch square cake tin with foil. Dissolve the sugar in milk over low heat. Bring to the boil and simmer for 10 minutes. Remove from heat and stir in the coconut. Pour half the mixture into the tin. Colour the other half pink and pour quickly over the first layer. Leave until slightly set, then mark into pieces and cut or break when cold.

Cookie faces

Makes 20 cookies
You will need:
★ 20 plain cookies
★ glacé icing
★ food colouring
★ selection of sweets, to decorate

Spread the icing on the cookies. Leave the icing to set for a few minutes, then add the sweet decorations.

Chocolate apples

Makes 4 apples
You will need:
★ 2 blocks chocolate cake covering (this will cover the fruit more easily than pure chocolate)
★ 4 lolly sticks
★ 4 eating apples
★ sweets and sprinkles, to decorate

Break the chocolate cake covering into pieces and melt in a heatproof bowl in the microwave for about 3–5 minutes on high. Or melt over a pan of simmering water, then remove from the heat. Push the sticks into the apples, then dip into the melted chocolate. Leave to harden slightly on foil, then decorate with sprinkles and sweets.

Brownies

Makes 12 brownies
You will need:
★ 175g/6oz plain chocolate
★ 125g/4oz unsalted butter
★ ½ tablespoon baking powder
★ 50g/2oz unsweetened cocoa powder
★ 4 large eggs
★ 300g/10oz caster sugar
★ ½ teaspoon almond essence
★ 1 teaspoon vanilla essence
★ 175g/6oz plain flour, sifted

Preheat the oven to 190°C/375°F/Gas Mark 5. Line a 23 x 28cm (9 x 11 inch) baking tin with silicone paper. Melt the chocolate, butter and cocoa powder in a heatproof bowl in the microwave on high for 1½ minutes, or over a pan of simmering water. Set aside to cool slightly. Whisk the eggs and add the sugar, almond and vanilla essence. Gently stir in the cooled chocolate mixture and add the flour, a little at a time. Pour the mixture into the tin and bake in the centre of the oven for 20–25 minutes. The outside should be firm and the inside slightly gooey. Remove from the oven and cool before cutting into portions. Dust with icing sugar before serving.

Chocolate biscuit lollipops

Makes 15 lollipops
You will need:
★ 250g/8oz butter
★ 50g/2oz caster sugar
★ 1 egg
★ 125g/4oz chocolate malt drinking powder, dissolved in 50ml/2 fl oz hot milk and cooled
★ 350g/12oz plain flour
★ 75g/3oz self-raising flour
★ 125g/4oz plain chocolate, grated
★ 15 lolly sticks
★ 175g/6oz each white and plain chocolate, melted
★ sprinkles and sweets

Heat oven to 180°C/350°F/Gas Mark 4. Line two baking trays with baking paper. Beat the butter, sugar and egg in a bowl till light and fluffy. Stir in the chocolate malt mixture, gradually add the flour and grated chocolate, then chill. Put the mixture on a lightly floured surface and roll until about 1cm/ ½ inch thick. Cut into lolly shapes about 4 x 8cm/1½ x 3½ inches and 1cm/½ inch thick. Transfer to baking sheets and insert the lolly sticks. Bake for 15 minutes, or until lightly coloured. Leave to cool for 5 minutes before transferring to a wire rack. Dip into melted white or plain chocolate and decorate with sprinkles and sweets before the chocolate sets completely.

Decorate your chocolate lollies with sprinkles and sweets.

Fruit pops

Makes 4 fruit pops
You will need:
★ 2 tubs of fruity fromage frais, such as strawberry and banana, or natural fromage frais with sugar to taste
★ small pieces of fruit of your choice
★ 4 lolly moulds

Push the lolly sticks into the moulds. Mix the fromage frais with your chosen fruit and spoon the mixture into the lolly moulds. Level the tops with a knife. Put the moulds in the freezer. Remove when the lollies are set, about 2–3 hours later, and then dip the bottom of the moulds in hot water to make it easier to remove the frozen fruit lollies.

Ginger shapes

Makes about 45 ginger shapes
You will need:

★ 1 tablespoon oil
★ 350g/12oz plain flour
★ 1 teaspoon bicarbonate of soda
★ 1 tablespoon ground ginger
★ 125g/4oz unsalted butter, cubed
★ 175g/6oz brown sugar
★ 1 egg
★ 4 tablespoons golden (corn) syrup
★ selection of sweets
★ glacé icing
★ ribbon

Heat oven to 190°C/375°F/Gas
Mark 5 and oil three baking sheets.
Mix flour, bicarbonate of soda
and ginger in a mixing bowl. Add
the butter and rub in with fingers
until mixture resembles fine
breadcrumbs. Add the sugar.
Mix the egg and golden syrup in a
separate bowl. Pour it into the flour
mixture and mix until it forms a
dough. Turn out on a floured surface
and knead for 5 minutes. Roll out
until about 1cm/½ inch thick, cut
into shapes and put on the baking
sheets. Bake for 15–20 minutes.
Allow to cool slightly, cut a
hole for the ribbon with a tiny
piping tube, and transfer to a wire
rack to cool. Decorate with glacé
icing and sweets and leave to set.

Thread ribbon
through the holes
and hang up your
ginger shapes.

Kids' cocktail time

Parties are thirsty work. Quench the children's thirst with these delicious drinks.

Hot chocolate

Makes 1 large mug
You will need:
★ 2 tablespoons cocoa powder
★ 3 tablespoons boiling water
★ 2 teaspoons sugar
★ 250ml/8 fl oz hot milk
★ marshmallows, to decorate

Dissolve the cocoa powder in the boiling water. Then stir in the sugar and the hot milk. Finally, top the hot chocolate with marshmallows.

Hot chocolate is bliss for budding chocolate lovers.

Pink lemonade

Makes 6 glasses
You will need:
★ juice of 6 fresh lemons
★ 500g/1lb ripe strawberries
★ 10 tablespoons sugar
★ 1.5 litres/2$\frac{1}{2}$ pints water

Blend together lemon juice, fruit and sugar. Pour into a jug and add water.

Real lemonade looks and tastes yummy.

Ice cream soda

Makes 2 glasses
You will need:
★ 300ml/$\frac{1}{2}$ pint lemonade
★ 125g/4oz mixed fresh fruit
★ 4 scoops ice cream

Set aside half of the mixed fruit. Put the rest of the ingredients into a blender and whizz until frothy. Pour out and decorate with skewers of mixed fruit, if you like.

Ice cream soda can also be made with cola.

Slurpies

Makes 4 glasses
You will need:

★ 350ml/12 fl oz mango juice
★ 350ml/12 fl oz diluted lime cordial
★ 350ml/12 fl oz diluted blackcurrant cordial

Freeze the juice and cordials in separate ice trays. Store in plastic bags. Blend the ice to a slush. Arrange coloured layers of ice in glasses.

You can serve slurpies with a straw or a spoon.

Banana shake

Makes 4 milkshakes
You will need:

★ 300ml/¹/₂ pint milk
★ 6 tablespoons double cream
★ 8 scoops vanilla ice cream
★ 2 bananas, sliced
★ 5 drops vanilla essence
★ drinking chocolate powder and chocolate sprinkles, to decorate

Put all the ingredients, apart from drinking chocolate and sprinkles, into a blender and whizz up till thick. Pour into chilled glasses and decorate.

Fruit cocktail

Makes 1 glass
You will need:

★ 175ml/6 fl oz lemonade
★ 125ml/4 fl oz mixed tropical fruit juice
★ 2 tablespoons grenadine syrup
★ 1 slice of pineapple
★ 1 glacé cherry
★ 1 cocktail stick

Half-fill a glass with lemonade. Tip the glass and very carefully pour the fruit juice down the side. Repeat with the grenadine syrup. Serve decorated with a pineapple slice and a cherry speared on a cocktail stick.

Make an exotic cocktail with tropical juice.

Making cocktails special

☆ **Serve in pretty glasses, available in different shapes and sizes.**
☆ **Use plastic glasses to avoid accidents.**
☆ **Decorate with cocktail stirrers and sticks.**
☆ **Serve with straws, which come in a range of styles and colours.**
☆ **Be generous with ice.**

Basic cake & cookie recipes

Victoria sponge

You will need:
- ★ 300g/10oz butter or margarine
- ★ 300g/10oz caster sugar
- ★ 5 medium eggs
- ★ 300g/10oz sifted self-raising flour

Preheat the oven to 180°C/350°F/ Gas Mark 4. Grease two 20cm/ 8 inch round cake tins. Cream the butter and sugar together in a mixing bowl until light and fluffy. Beat in the eggs, one at a time, then slowly add the sifted flour. Pour the mixture into the prepared tins and bake for 35–40 minutes, or until the surface of the cake springs back when pressed. Leave to cool in the cake tin for 5 minutes, then turn out on to a wire rack.

Flavourings
- ☆ **Coffee:** dissolve 1 tablespoon of instant coffee in 1 tablespoon of hot water, and add after the flour.
- ☆ **Chocolate:** dissolve 2 tablespoons of cocoa powder in 2 tablespoons of hot water, and add after the flour.
- ☆ **Lemon:** add the grated rind of a lemon and 1 tablespoon of juice.

Madeira cake

You will need:
* ★ 175g/6oz butter
* ★ 175g/6oz sugar
* ★ 3 eggs
* ★ 250g/8oz sifted self-raising flour
* ★ 2 tablespoons milk

Preheat the oven to 160°C/325°F/Gas Mark 3 and grease a 1kg/2lb loaf tin. Cream the butter and sugar together in a bowl until light and fluffy. Beat in the eggs, one at a time, adding a little flour if the mixture starts to curdle. Fold in the rest of the flour. Add enough milk to form a dropping consistency. Pour the mixture into the prepared tin and bake for 1–1¼ hours, or until the sponge springs back when pressed. Remove the cake from the oven, and allow it to cool for 5 minutes. Then turn the cake out on to a wire rack and allow it to cool completely.

Crumbs!

Victoria and Madeira sponge cakes are much better when they are baked the day before they are iced, as they will then be a lot firmer and less likely to crumble when they are cut.

This cake has been iced with ready-to-roll white icing, which is available in blocks from supermarkets.

A very simple way of decorating a cake is to use a selection of silver balls and colourful sweets.

Carrot cake

You will need:

★ 125g/4oz self-raising flour
★ 1 teaspoon cinnamon
★ pinch of grated nutmeg
★ $1/2$ teaspoon salt
★ 300g/10oz soft brown sugar
★ 250ml/8 fl oz vegetable oil
★ 3 large eggs, beaten
★ 300g/10oz grated carrots
★ 175g/6oz chopped walnuts
   (optional)
★ butter for greasing the cake tin

Preheat the oven to 180°C/350°F/Gas
Mark 4. Grease and line a 25cm/10 inch round
cake tin. Sift the flour, spices and salt into a large
bowl. Mix the sugar and oil in another bowl, then
add the eggs. Make a well in the flour, stir in the
liquid, then add the carrots and the walnuts, if using.
Spoon the mixture into the tin and bake for $1-1\frac{1}{4}$
hours, or until a skewer inserted into the cake comes
out cleanly. Allow to cool in the tin, then turn out on
a wire rack.

This cake is iced
with a lemon cream
cheese topping and
decorated with
marzipan carrots.

A nutty choice

**Try using almonds instead of
walnuts. But always check
that no one is allergic to nuts.**

Buttercream

You will need:

★ 50g/2oz unsalted butter
★ 125g/4oz sifted icing sugar

Cream the butter and icing sugar
together in a bowl. Buttercream
can be used either between layers
of sponge or on top of the cake,
as preferred. It is very rich – and
deliciously wicked!

Glacé icing

You will need:

★ 250g/8oz sifted icing sugar
★ 3–4 tablespoons hot water

Put the icing sugar in a bowl and
pour on the hot water, mixing as
you do so, until the icing leaves a
ribbon trail on itself when the
spoon is lifted. Food colouring
can then be added if wished.

Lemon topping

You will need:

★ 250g/8oz cream cheese
★ grated rind of $1/2$ lemon
★ 25g/1oz icing sugar

Mix together the cream cheese
and lemon rind, and stir in the
icing sugar. Spoon the mixture
over the cake and smooth it over
with a palette knife.

Cookie dough

You will need:

- ★ 125g/4oz unsalted butter, plus a little extra to grease the baking sheets
- ★ 125g/4oz caster sugar
- ★ 175g/6oz plain flour, plus a little extra for rolling out
- ★ 1 egg, beaten
- ★ pinch of salt
- ★ 1 teaspoon vanilla essence

Preheat the oven to 180°C/350°F/Gas Mark 4. Beat the butter and sugar together until light and fluffy. Sift the flour into the bowl. Add the egg, salt and vanilla essence, and mix well. Knead the dough for a few minutes until it forms a ball. To make cookies, pinch off 12 small pieces of dough and roll each one into a ball. Place the balls, well apart, on a greased baking tray and flatten each one a little with your fingertips. Bake the cookies for 12–15 minutes or until light golden brown.

Flavourings

To make chocolate chip cookies, add 125g/4oz of chocolate chips along with the vanilla essence.

Gingerbread

You will need:

- ★ 350g/12oz plain flour
- ★ 1 teaspoon bicarbonate of soda
- ★ 1 tablespoon ground ginger
- ★ 125g/4oz butter
- ★ 175g/6oz soft brown sugar
- ★ 1 egg
- ★ 4 tablespoons golden syrup

Preheat oven to 180°C/350°F/Gas Mark 4. Mix the flour, bicarbonate of soda and ginger in a bowl. Rub in butter till mixture resembles fine breadcrumbs. Beat together egg and syrup in a separate bowl, then add to flour mixture and mix until it forms a ball. Knead on a floured work surface. Chill in fridge for 1 hour. Roll out to required thickness and cut into shapes. Bake for 10–15 minutes according to size.

Novelty cakes

Butterfly cake

You will need:

★ 1 Victoria sponge,
   made with 4 eggs and
   250g/8oz each of self-
   raising flour, caster
   sugar and butter, and
   baked in a 23cm/9
   inch round cake tin
★ buttercream icing,
   made using 250g/8oz

★ butter and 500g/
   1lb icing sugar
★ pink, blue, yellow
   and green food
   colouring
★ 1 large Swiss roll
★ a selection of sweets,
   for decoration
★ 2 birthday candle
   holders and 2 candles

Cut the cake in half and make cuts into the sides to
form wings, as shown. Arrange the Swiss roll in
between the two wings to form the butterfly's body.
Make the buttercream icing and divide into 4

separate bowls for the different colours. Colour most
of the icing pink, and the rest blue, yellow and green.
Cover the cake with pink icing. Spread yellow, blue
and green icing on top of the pink icing and mix
together, forming a rainbow pattern. Decorate with
sweets and arrange candle holders and candles at the
top of the cake to form antennae.

Volcano cake

You will need:

★ 2 chocolate cakes – 1
   made in a 900ml/1¹/₂
   pint pudding basin
   and 1 made in a mini
   basin, using a basic
   Madeira cake recipe

★ chocolate
   buttercream
★ orange glacé icing
★ a selection of sweets,
   to decorate
★ sparklers (optional)

Place the mini pudding basin cake on top of the
larger cake and cut to form a volcano shape. Hollow
out a crater. Cover the cake with chocolate
buttercream and a few sweets to look like molten
lava. Add the orange glacé icing to form the flow
of lava. Stick in a few red, orange and yellow
sweets to look like molten boulders.

For a touch of
drama, light three
cake sparklers
in the volcano's
crater.

Rocket cake

You will need:

★ 4 chocolate-covered Swiss rolls
★ chocolate cake covering, melted
★ 2 mini chocolate Swiss rolls
★ 6 fan wafers
★ plain chocolate, melted
★ coloured balls, sprinkles and sweets, to decorate
★ 1 ice-cream cone

Stand 3 Swiss rolls together on a cake board and secure them with melted chocolate cake covering. Place the fourth Swiss roll on top of the others and again secure with chocolate, then arrange the mini chocolate Swiss rolls around the bottom, as shown in the picture.

Dip the fan wafers into the melted chocolate, then stick coloured balls on the edges. Place the wafers around the rocket as shown. Dip the ice-cream cone in chocolate, place upside down on top of the rocket, and cover in sprinkles. Decorate with piped-on lines and stick on coloured sweets with chocolate, as shown.

The imaginative use of sweets, balls and sprinkles is an effective way of decorating cakes.

Assembly

You don't have to be an accomplished cake maker to produce some very impressive novelty cakes. Simply assembling bought, ready-made cakes, such as Swiss rolls, and decorating them with melted chocolate, icing and sweets can be just as effective.

Princess castle cake

You will need:

★ **2 large Swiss rolls, cut in half horizontally to make the four towers**

★ **250–350g/8–12 oz buttercream icing**

★ **3 Battenberg cakes**

★ **4 ice-cream cones**

★ **1 packet mini-Battenberg cakes, cut into squares**

★ **a selection of sweets, silver balls, jelly diamonds and sprinkles, to decorate**

Cover each Swiss roll in pink buttercream. Assemble the large Battenberg cakes, cutting off a small triangle from each corner, and the Swiss rolls into a square castle. Cover the cones with icing and then roll in the sprinkles. Leave to set. Decorate the castle with miniature Battenberg crenellations, ice-cream cone towers, and sweets, securing them all with buttercream.

A fragile cake like this is best made on the board where it will remain throughout the party.

A door made from wafers and a path and windows made from jelly diamonds are nice finishing touches.

Treasure chest cake

You will need:
- ★ 1 chocolate Madeira cake made in a 1kg/2lb loaf tin
- ★ chocolate buttercream icing
- ★ yellow marzipan
- ★ a selection of sweets

Cut the top third off the cake to form the lid. Gouge a hollow inside the chest. Spread the insides with chocolate frosting and fill the chest with sweets – preferably ones that look like jewels. Re-assemble the cake. Cover the outside with chocolate frosting and smooth with a palette knife dipped in hot water. Roll the marzipan into a long thin sheet and cut it into narrow strips. Lay them on the chest, pressing them gently into the frosting.

Angelfish cake

You will need:
- ★ 1 Madeira or Victoria sponge, flavoured with the grated zest and juice of 1 lemon and a pinch of cinnamon, and baked in a 23cm/9 inch round cake tin
- ★ 3 x 250g/8oz blocks of ready-to-roll white icing
- ★ blue, green and yellow food colouring
- ★ apricot glaze
- ★ a selection of sweets, to decorate

Cut out cake shapes for the fish, as shown in the picture. Colour the three blocks of ready-to-roll icing yellow, green and blue. Brush the cake with warmed apricot glaze. Roll out the icing on a surface sprinkled with icing sugar, one colour at a time, and cover the body with yellow and blue stripes and the face, tail and fins with the green icing. Don't forget to carry the icing on over the sides of the cake. Decorate the fish with sweets for the eyes and mouth, and little blobs of blue icing to suggest bubbles.

Knead in enough food colouring, using clean rubber gloves, for the desired intensity.

Football cake

You will need:

★ I quantity of basic Madeira cake, made in a 600ml/I pint pudding basin and baked for 50 minutes at 180°C/350°F/ Gas Mark 4
★ ready-to-roll white icing
★ blue food colouring
★ apricot glaze

Turn out the cake and trim to make a ball shape. Roll out half the white icing and cut into hexagons. Colour the remaining icing blue, roll out and cut into hexagons. Brush the cake with a thin layer of apricot glaze and, starting with a blue hexagon at the top, arrange the hexagons on the cake. If you like, you can outline the definition between hexagons with an icing pen, as shown.

To remove ice cream from tin, soak a tea towel in hot water, wring out and wrap around tin.

You must work fast because the ice cream melts quickly.

Cactus cake

You will need:

★ 3 litres/5 pints ice cream
★ mint chocolate sticks
★ desiccated coconut
★ a few drops of green food colouring to colour coconut

Spoon the ice cream into a 23cm/9 inch round loose-bottomed cake tin. Smooth with a palette knife. Return to the freezer till solid. Meanwhile, cut out a cardboard template of a cactus. Take the ice cream out of the freezer and remove it from the tin. Cut out the cactus shape quickly, and put the cut-out shape back in the freezer till solid. Remove from freezer, push chocolate sticks into the ice cream to resemble cactus spines, and sprinkle with green desiccated coconut. Return to the freezer until you are ready to serve.

Farmhouse cake

You will need:

★ **3 quantities gingerbread dough**
★ **250g/8oz glacé or royal icing**
★ **buttercream icing**
★ **food colouring**
★ **sweets, for decoration**

Make up cardboard templates and cut out the shapes for the farmhouse. Heat the oven to 180°C/350°F/Gas Mark 4. Roll out the gingerbread and cut to the desired shapes. Transfer to a cookie sheet lined with baking parchment. Bake in the top of the oven in batches for 12–15 minutes. Place on a rack to cool. Cut out animal shapes, put in oven and bake for 7–10 minutes. Remove and cool on a rack. Stick the farmhouse together with icing, starting with the walls, then the roof and the chimney. Decorate the animal shapes with icing in different colours. Assemble the farmyard scene on a board covered in green buttercream icing.

Farmhouse cake templates

A wisp of cotton-wool smoke coming out of the chimney gives the farmhouse a homely air.

Cookie clown

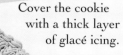

You will need:

★ 1 quantity of chocolate chip cookie dough

★ 1 quantity of white glacé icing

★ coloured, ready-to-roll moulding icing

★ sweets

Heat the oven to 180°C/350°F/Gas Mark 4. Roll the cookie dough into a large circle about 3cm/1¼ inch deep, using a plate as a guide. Transfer it to a greased baking tray and bake for 20 minutes. Transfer the cookie to a wire rack to cool.

Cover the cookie with a thick layer of glacé icing.

Making faces

This cookie is decorated with a clown's face, but you could also make a cat, a rabbit or even someone you know!

Make a mouth and nose using coloured moulding icing and decorate with sweets.

Numbers

Celebrate a birthday in style with a special cake made in the shape of the birthday child's age. This is, in fact, surprisingly easy to do. Simply use one or two Madeira sponge cakes in the shapes and sizes detailed here...

You will need:
2 loaf cakes (each 25 x 8cm/10 x 3½ inches)

You will need:
1 rectangular cake (28 x 18cm/11 x 7 inches); 1 loaf cake (25 x 8cm/10 x 3½ inches)

You will need:
2 ring cakes (each 20cm/ 8 inches)

You will need:
1 rectangular cake (28 x 18cm/11 x 7 inches)

Polly parrot

You will need:

★ I quantity of plain cookie dough
★ pale green glacé icing
★ candy-coated chocolate drops
  or jelly beans
★ dark green glacé icing

Preheat the oven to 180°C/350°F/Gas
Mark 4. Roll out the cookie dough into
a rectangle about 30 x 15cm/12 x 6
inches. Lay the dough on a
baking sheet and bake for
25 minutes. Cool slightly
and then, using a template,
cut a parrot and branch
shapes from the dough. Use
the off-cuts to shape some leaves.

When the cookie is cool,
spread over the pale green
glacé icing. Then, using the
picture as a guide, decorate
the parrot with sweets.

Other shapes

We've made a cookie
parrot – and jolly
splendid he looks – but
there is no reason why
you can't make any
other shapes that take
your fancy – a cat, say,
or a train, or a boat.
Simply choose any of
your child's favourite
things and make up
your own template.

Cover the branches
and leaves with dark
green glacé icing.

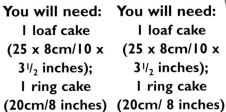

You will need:
I loaf cake
(25 x 8cm/10 x
3¹/₂ inches);
I ring cake
(20cm/8 inches)

You will need:
I loaf cake (25
x 8cm/10 x 3¹/₂
inches); I ring
cake (20cm/8
inches)

You will need:
2 loaf cakes
(25 x 8cm/10 x
3¹/₂ inches)

You will need:
I large ring
cake (20cm/8
inches); I small
ring cake
(15cm/6 inches)

You will need:
I loaf cake
(25 x 8cm/10 x
3¹/₂ inches);
I ring cake
(20cm/8 inches)

You will need:
I loaf cake
(25 x 8cm/10 x
3¹/₂ inches);
I ring cake
(20cm/ 8 inches)

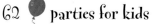

Breaking the ice

The first half-hour of any party can be awkward. Some children may not know anyone, and some may be shy. Children will arrive at slightly different times, which can be difficult for the newcomer.

The name game

Before the party, write out the names of each guest on a piece of card. Colour the letters and cut out each one. Then prepare another strip of card with a piece of sticky-back Velcro attached to the back. Finally, make a chart of all the children's names and pin this to the wall – just in case they don't know how to spell their names. Scatter the letters throughout the room and, as the children arrive, ask them to hunt for the letters of their name. Once they have found them, ask them to stick them on to the piece of card with Velcro on the back to make their own name badge.

Hunting for stars

You will need a packet of little stars. The tiny thumbnail size are the best ones to use. Hide them around the room before the party begins, bearing in mind that they should be within the children's reach and how difficult they are to find should depend on the children's age. The idea is that the children collect as many pairs – two stars of the same colour – as they can, and the person who finds the most wins.

Colour a hat

Cut out hat shapes and put them on the table with crayons or felt-tipped pens for the kids to colour in. The hats can be themed to match the party, or just jolly ones that the children can make themselves.

Silly hats help break the ice.

Rogues' gallery

You may need a helper with this game, depending on the age of the children, as those that are less able will probably need some assistance. Prepare a craft table, with lots of paper or crayons and felt-tipped pens, and ask the children to draw their own self-portrait. As they finish the drawing, ask them to write their name on the back and pin it up on the wall, or on a board. Each one wins a prize.

Where's the honey pot?

Paint a large picture of a woodland scene. On the back, draw a honey pot, and check that this is visible from the front when you hold the picture up to the light. Write each child's name on a teddy card, and tell the children to position the teddy where they think the honey pot is hidden, using putty or double-sided sticky tape. When each child has had a go, hold the picture up to the light to see whose teddy is closest.

The wool trail

Tie a chocolate bar to different-coloured balls of wool – one for each of the guests. Hide the chocolate and gently unravel the wool around the room, trying not to tangle the different colours. Lay a more or less complicated route according to the age of the guests. As they arrive, give each child a piece of wool to match their ball, and ask them to start searching.

Variations on a theme

Other things to draw could be a teddy, a cat, or a car, depending on their age and their interests.

It's difficult to be in a bad mood when you're wearing a funny hat.

A hat can make a child feel special.

Children love dressing up in hats from a very early age.

Noisy games

There's nothing quite like a good noisy game for letting off steam. As long as you can stand the noise, here are a few suggestions for having a lot of fun.

Fish in the sea

This is a good chasing game for a confined space. Sit the children down in a circle, facing inwards. Choose the names of three fish and walk round the circle, naming the children in sequence – cod, mackerel and shark, cod, mackerel and shark, and so on. You then have several of each fish sitting at intervals. Explain that, when their name is called, the fish have to get up and go for a swim. This entails walking clockwise round the outside of the circle and listening to what happens. Talk them through the game: when you say the sea is rough, they run; when you say it's getting rougher, they run faster; when you say the tide turns, they turn and run in the other direction; and when you shout 'STORM', they have to run back to their original spaces. The last to arrive is out and has to sit in the circle facing outwards.

Musical cushions

For this game, you need a cassette player and a cushion for each child playing. Scatter the cushions on the floor. While the music plays, the players walk or dance around the room. Once it stops, each child must sit on a cushion with no part of their body touching the floor. At the start of each new round, one cushion is removed. The player who finds him- or herself stranded without a cushion once the music stops is out. The last player left wins the game.

Musical dressing up

Make a collection of clothes that the children can put on. Decorate four boxes, each one with a different colour. Put one in each corner of the room and fill it with some clothes in the same colour as the box. Play music for the children to dance to. When the music stops, they have to run to whichever colour you call and put on something from the box. When all the clothes have been used up, hold a fashion parade to see what everyone looks like.

Flying saucers

The players all dance around in a circle to lively music. When the leader calls, 'Flying saucers sit down in twos' (or threes or fours...), everyone rushes to get into a group of the number called. Those who are last to sit down or who are left out of a group are out. The last two left in the game are the winners.

Crossing the river

Stretch a length of lining paper or wallpaper across the centre of the room. This represents the river that the children have to run across while you play music. Anyone who is in the river when the music stops is considered to have 'drowned'. The winner is the last one to be left 'alive'.

On the stroke of midnight

This game requires plenty of space. The children dance to music until you clang a saucepan lid loudly to announce the approach of midnight. At this point, all the children rush to a given spot, or through an open door, or leap on to the sofa – whatever you have told them they should do. The last child to do this is out. Repeat the music and 'chimes' until only one child is left – who is the winner.

Spiders and flies

This is a very lively game, which children really enjoy. One person is 'it', or the spider. He or she rushes around crying out, 'I need some flies for my web,' and tries to catch as many children – who run around being the flies – as possible. Once a fly has been caught, he or she has to stand still with legs apart, until released by one of the other flies who hasn't been caught. To do this, he or she has to crawl between the legs of the child who is the fly caught in the web. This can go on for a long time, so put a time limit on it to enable other children to have a go at being the spider.

Quiet games

There are moments at virtually every party when the children become overexcited after playing noisy games. This is the time to calm them down by playing some quiet games such as these.

Pass-the-parcel

Although this game has music, it is an excellent one for calming children down when they have been very active. Choose as many little prizes, such as sweets or felt-tipped pens, as there are guests, plus one larger one for the main prize. Wrap all the prizes in several layers of newspaper or old wrapping paper, beginning with the main prize. The children sit in a circle and pass the parcel round to each other. When the music stops, they have to unwrap as many layers as possible in order to win a prize before the music starts again. When playing this game with young children, watch what is happening carefully and try to make sure that every child wins a prize.

Pass-the-parcel is a traditional favourite for children of all ages.

Memory game

This can be as simple or as difficult as you like, depending on the age of the children. To take part in this, the children must be able to write quite well. Arrange some toys on a tray and cover them with a cloth. Give each child a piece of paper and a pencil. Remove the cloth and give the children 60 seconds to memorize as many of the items as possible. They then have to write down as many of the items as they can. The child who remembers the most items correctly is the winner.

Variations on a theme

Show the children a tray of goodies for 60 seconds. Then remove some of the items and ask them to write down what's missing.

Grandmother's footsteps

Choose one player to be the grandmother. She stands with her back to the other players, with a prize next to her. The players must creep up on her while her back is turned. When she turns round to look – which she can do as often as she likes – the players must freeze and stand as still as statues. If she sees someone moving, she points to the player and that person is out. The winner is the first person to reach the prize without the grandmother seeing him or her move.

Variations on a theme

This game can be adapted for themed parties. For the Spooky party, for example, the grandmother can be a witch; for the Space party, she can be an alien; or for the Wild West party, she can be a sheriff.

Sleeping lions

Choose someone to be 'it'. All the children lie down and become sleeping lions. They lie flat on their backs and have to keep as still as possible – and absolutely no giggling allowed! The 'it' person has to try to make them laugh by pulling funny faces but not actually touching them. Anyone who is found giggling is out. The last lion left in is the winner.

Variations on a theme

This game can easily be adapted to suit any of the themed parties – for example, Sleeping clowns, Sleeping astronauts, Sleeping pirates, Sleeping cowboys, or whatever appeals to your child most.

Team games

Children can become confused as to which team they belong to. Have each team wear a different-coloured band, badge or hat to help identify them.

Flapping fish

This is a team relay race. Cut a fish shape from tissue paper for each team. The children must fan their fish along the ground with a newspaper from one line to another. The first one over the finishing line wins. The children must flap their fish round a chair and back to their team for the next player to have a go.

Who am I ?

This game is similar to charades, but the children have to mime a famous person. They should define which categories the people come from, the most obvious ones being cinema, sport, pop, theatre and television. Divide the children into two teams.

Boat race

Divide the children into teams of about six. They sit in a line with their legs wide apart and with their arms around the waist of the person in front. When you say 'go', all the crew must shuffle their bottoms to move themselves forward, but the line must not be broken or the team must start again. The winning team is the first across the finishing line.

Mackerel on the line

This team relay race can be played in a relatively confined space, wherever there is somewhere suitable to suspend two washing lines. Put ten pegs on each line. Stand the team in a starting position some distance away. The first child in each team runs to the line, unpegs the pegs (mackerel) as fast as possible, and runs and hands them to the second child who runs and pegs them back on the line again (the bait) and so on until everyone has had a turn. To make it more difficult for older children, you can penalize them for dropping any pegs by removing these from the game. The winning team is the one that has caught the most mackerel.

Plate race

Mark out a river, about 2 metres (6½ feet) wide, across the centre of the room. Divide each team so that half the members are sitting on either side of the river. The first child in each team holds two paper plates and when you say 'go', they have to cross the river using the plates as stepping stones. They put down the first plate and step on it, then put the next plate ahead while standing on one foot and step on that one, then lift the back foot and move the original plate forwards and so on (not as easy as it sounds!). When they reach the other side, they hand the plates to the first person in the line, who crosses back again.

Googly ballons behave in a delightfully unpredictable way.

Googly balloons

Blow up balloons, putting a marble through the neck of each one before you tie the end. This weights the balloons and makes them behave in unexpected ways. Release into the group one more balloon than children. The object is to keep the balloons up in the air. Play this in two teams, each side with an extra balloon. The team who lets a balloon drop to the floor first loses. Great fun!

This game will make children quite hysterical with laughter.

Outdoor games & activities

When the children need to run around and let off steam, plan an outside activity party, either in the garden or in the park. But remember – it would be unwise to give them their tea before all that boisterous exercise!

Crab race

You need plenty of room for this race – a large lawn is ideal. Line up the children in a row and show them how to grasp their ankles and run like a crab. Arrange a finishing line not more than 10 metres (11 yards) away. Any child who lets go of his or her ankles or falls over is automatically out of the race. The winner is the first child over the line.

Wheelbarrow race

This is another race that is run in pairs. One person stands in front of the other. The person at the back lifts the legs of the person in front, while the person in front puts his or hands on the ground to bear their weight. They then run the race in this position.

3-legged race

The children pair off with a partner, and tie their centre legs together with a scarf. They then have to run the race with 'three legs'. Pairs of a similar height and build tend to be the best, though the sight of one small and one large pairing can be very amusing.

The spud-and-spoon race makes a lot less mess than an egg-and-spoon race but is just as much fun.

Spud-and-spoon race

This is a variation on the traditional egg-and-spoon race. The children have to run an allotted distance carrying a small potato balanced on a spoon. If the potato falls off the spoon, the child must pick it up without his or her fingers touching the potato and start all over again.

Balancing a potato on a spoon needs concentration.

Sack race

Each competitor climbs into a large sack and races by jumping along with their feet in the sack. Any large bag will do, but plastic bin liners are ideal. Make sure no one puts his or her head in the bag.

Obstacle race

Plan an obstacle course before the race begins, including fun things like crawling under a blanket, hopping along a plank propped up on two flowerpots, skipping ten times, turning a somersault, and so on. If you are in a garden, you may be able to try more adventurous things like swinging on a rope from a tree. Include about six to ten activities and show the children what they must do before the race begins.

Bobbing for corks

This a very wet game and obviously best played outside. It is strictly for volunteers only! Put a bowl, half-full of water, on the floor and place several corks in it. Tell the children to retrieve the corks without using their hands – and keep a towel handy for mopping wet faces!

Flowerpot race

Each of the competitors has a pair of flowerpots. When the 'go' is given, they each step on to one of them and put the other pot in front, without allowing the free foot to touch the ground. They then step on to the front flowerpot and balance on this one, reaching back to lift the pot behind and put that one in front. Anyone who loses their balance and falls over has to start all over again.

Games for the very young

Below are some suggestions for suitable games for very young children. All the games require careful supervision by an adult, who can direct proceedings and make sure that no one cheats!

Tommy

This is a very simple game but never fails to delight children. You need a dish of candy-covered chocolates. One person is 'it' and has to leave the room, while the others choose a colour to be Tommy. The child returns and eats a sweetie out of the dish. If no one says anything, he or she takes another colour, and another, until he or she takes the colour that is Tommy, at which point all the children call out and some-one else is chosen to be 'it'.

Cats and dogs

Before the party begins, scatter a selection of brightly coloured buttons or counters around the house and, if the weather is fine, the garden. Divide the children into two teams – these are the cats and dogs. Each team has an adult leader. The object of the game is to find all the buttons or counters. When each one is found, the cats miaow to call their leader, and the dogs bark to call theirs, as only the leaders can pick them up. The team that has the most buttons or counters at the end of the game wins, and each team member should be given a prize.

Squeak!

First of all, the player who is 'it' is given a cushion and then blindfolded. All the other children sit in a circle on the floor. The child who is 'it' is turned round three times, and then has to find a player, put the cushion on their lap, and sit on it. He or she calls out, 'Squeak, Piggy, Squeak' and the squashed player underneath must squeak very loudly. If the person who is 'it' can name the squeaker, they then swap places. If not, they have to find someone else to sit on until they can identify the squeak. Whenever someone new takes over as 'it', the other players must all change places in the circle, after the blindfold has been put on.

What's the time, Mr Wolf?

This is a game of chase and catch. The wolf is the chaser and the children are his prey. There is a safe place – a sofa or space in the room. The children follow the wolf around the room calling out, 'What's the time, Mr Wolf?' If he replies with any time such as 'one o'clock', they are safe. But as soon as he calls out 'dinner time', they have to run for safety. Anyone who is caught can take the place of Mr Wolf.

In and out of the bluebells

The children stand in a circle with a space between each one of them and an adult as the leader. They all sing this song together:

In and out the dusty bluebells
In and out the dusty bluebells
In and out the dusty bluebells
Who will be my partner?

Tippy tippy tap tap on my shoulder
Tippy tippy tap tap on my shoulder
Tippy tippy tap tap on my shoulder
You will be my partner.

The leader taps a child on the shoulder and that child puts his or her hands on the leader's shoulder or waist (depending on height). The two of them weave in and out of the circle, singing the song, and choose another child. And so on until all the children are joined together.

Lost teddy

Stand the children in a large circle facing inwards – all except for one child who is holding a teddy in his or her arms. This child now walks outside the circle in an anticlockwise direction and drops the teddy behind another child of his or her choosing. The second child picks up the teddy and races the first child round the circle to sit in the vacated space. The child who is left standing then walks outside the circle in an anticlockwise direction and drops the teddy behind another child of his or her choosing – and the next round begins. The game continues in this way until all the children have had a turn.

Going-home presents

Every child who's invited to a party nowadays expects to go home with a party bag full of goodies. Sorting out all the going-home presents is therefore an essential part of organizing the party.

Going-home presents after a party can add a tremendous additional expense to what is already quite a costly event. But with a little bit of imagination, you can cut the cost considerably and still give the children something really special to take home with them.

Homemade presents

There are a great many things that you can make for the children's going-home presents. What you make depends on whether your skills lie in the cookery or the crafts field. Ideas include:

★ cookies
★ candies
★ marzipan animals
★ chocolate apples
★ purses
★ key rings
★ badges
★ papier-mâché jewellery
★ masks
★ hats

Can I help?

Kids love making up party bags for their friends to take home.

Buying presents

Toy shops, party shops, stationery shops, newsagents, even supermarkets – they all offer a wide range of things you can buy for party bags. To prevent it all getting too expensive, set yourself a limit – say, £1 or £1.50 per bag. That may sound like a tall order but you'll be surprised at how cheaply you can fill a party bag.

★ pens, pencils, crayons
★ mini-chocolate bars
★ stickers
★ playing cards and dice
★ books and notebooks
★ soaps and shower gel
★ bags of sweets
★ personalized balloons
★ bead kits
★ face paints
★ hair ornaments
★ jewellery
★ badges
★ colouring books
★ pencil sharpeners
★ rubbers
★ mini-cheeses
★ packets of seeds
★ bubble kits
★ shells
★ fans

Traditionally, the Mexican piñata is brightly coloured and made in the shape of a donkey.

Papier-mâché piñata

How the going-home presents are presented is important, and something a bit different from the usual goody bag from the local toy shop will add greatly to the excitement.

In Mexico, a piñata is a traditional party decoration. It is made out of papier-mâché and is filled with sweets and small gifts. The traditional Mexican piñata is made in the shape of a donkey, but you can make one in any shape you like, according to the theme of the party – a fish, a flower, a fairy, an animal, or whatever your child would like. It is hung up as a decoration throughout the party and then, when the fun and games are over, the children hit it with a stick until it breaks open and all the sweets and presents come tumbling out.

For many kids, a major part of the fun is the goody bag that they're given after the party.

Making a piñata

You will need:

★ large balloon
★ PVA glue
★ scraps of newspaper
★ poster paints
★ cellophane, tissue or crêpe paper
★ craft knife
★ string
★ selection of sweets and little presents

1 Blow up a large balloon and tie the neck in a double knot.

2 Cover the balloon with a layer of newspaper strips. To do this, first apply a dab of glue and stick on a strip of newspaper, then apply another dab of glue and stick on another strip of newspaper and so on, until the balloon is completely covered in layers of newspaper strips and is itself invisible.

3 Repeat the whole process until the balloon has at least three layers of newspaper around it. Allow the glue to dry thoroughly – this will take as long as one or two days, depending on how many layers of newspaper and glue you have applied.

4 Paint the piñata with poster paint in bright colours. Decorate with cellophane, tissue or crêpe paper streamers.

5 When the piñata is completely dry, cut a small opening in the top of it. Prick the balloon and remove it. Make a couple of holes with the knife on either side of the opening and thread through the string for hanging up. Finally, fill the hollow with a selection of sweets and little presents.

Countdown

There always seems to be so much to do and never enough time to do it in. Organization is the answer. Keep a countdown to the big day handy and avoid any last-minute panic. Good luck!

4 weeks to go...

★ Select party theme and venue.
★ Decide on the number of guests and make a list.
★ Decide on your helpers.
★ Make and send the invitations.
★ Book the entertainer, if you are having one.

3 weeks to go...

★ Organize transport to the venue.
★ Make the piñata (see page 75), and any homemade going-home presents.

2 weeks to go...

★ Buy or make any decorations or props.
★ Buy paper plates and cups, napkins, balloons, candles, and cake board.
★ Make the costumes.
★ Plan the games and make a list.
★ Choose the music.

1 week to go...

★ Buy non-perishable ingredients for the food.
★ Buy any ready-made going-home presents and prizes.

3 days to go...

★ Baking day: make the cookies and birthday cake.
★ Sort out party clothes, and wash and iron them.

2 days to go...

★ Make iced items for the freezer.

1 day to go...

★ Decorate the house and table.
★ Organize the first aid kit.
★ Buy all the perishable items of food.
★ Wrap up going-home presents.
★ Fill the piñata.
★ Wrap up pass-the-parcel.

8 hours to go...

★ Prepare the games.

2 hours to go...

★ Make the fresh food and drink.
★ Blow up the balloons.
★ Put a sign and balloons on the gate or front door to show guests where the party is.

1 hour to go...

★ Set the table.
★ Put out the food.

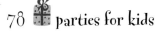

Your problems solved

Above all, parties should be fun, but they're not without their problems. We have the answers to some of the most common ones.

My daughter is six and her whole class at school is usually invited to parties. I just don't have the space.

You could take all the children out – to an inexpensive restaurant, say, for a pizza or a hamburger. Or just tell your daughter that you do not have the room and she can invite just six of her best friends. She won't get as many presents, but you won't have as much hassle.

I can't afford the birthday present my child has his heart set on. What can I do?

Tell him the truth. Parties and birthdays are expensive occasions. One solution might be to say that you can afford to buy half of it and maybe he can contribute the other half through savings and odd jobs. Or you could ask all the relatives to contribute to one big, much-wanted gift.

My elder daughter is jealous that her younger sister is having a party. How do I help her overcome these feelings?

A good way to deal with this problem is to include your elder daughter in the preparations for the party and ask her to organize some of the games. She'll feel a lot better if she feels involved.

My son wants his dad (my ex-husband) at his birthday party. We have hardly spoken since the divorce settlement, and I really don't want him there. Am I being unfair?

It is important for your child to have a relationship with his father. Make sure that his father knows all the details – when, where, etc. Next, stress that it would be better if he came on his own. And lastly, find out exactly when he is arriving so your son won't be disappointed. There's nothing wrong with putting an ending time on it too – after all, the other guests have been given one.

I do not get on with my mother-in-law. She is so bossy and insensitive, but I feel it is important for her to be part of all our family celebrations. What should I do?

The best way to deal with this situation is to involve your mother-in-law in some way. Ask her to help with the tea for the adults, say, or to be in charge of taking the children to the loo.

I do not have time to make going-home presents for the children who are coming to the party. What can I buy for them instead, and how much will I need to spend?

There are plenty of options for you to choose from. You should expect to spend at least £1 to £1.50 on each child. For this amount you can buy a fairly substantial toy, or a selection of pencils, beads or shells. When you buy in bulk, you can always ask for a discount. You can also include a few mini-size chocolate bars.

First aid

With so many children running about, minor accidents can happen. Keep a list of contact telephone numbers handy in case of an emergency. Below is a quick reference guide for dealing with partytime mishaps.

Bruises: Raise the bruised area and apply a cold compress in the form of an ice pack or frozen peas.

Dry burns and scalds: Immerse the injury in cold water for ten minutes. Remove any constricting clothing and apply a dry, preferably sterile dressing.

Fainting: Lay the child down, with legs raised, and ensure the airway is clear by loosening any clothes at the neck, chest and waist. Check for injury.

Foreign bodies in the eye: If the foreign body is embedded, seek medical help. If the child has dust or a loose eyelash in the eye, sit the child in a chair facing the light. Stand behind the child, with his or her head resting against you. Gently separate the eyelids with your index finger and thumb and flood the eye with water (preferably sterile) using an eye-bath to wash out the foreign body. Or lift it out with the corner of a clean, damp hanky.

Grazes: Clean the area under running water. Protect the wound with a sterile dressing while you clean the surrounding area, then cover with a plaster.

Stings: For a sting in the mouth, give the child ice cubes to suck and seek help. For a sting elsewhere, remove it with tweezers and apply a cold compress.

Nosebleeds: Sit the child down with his or her head leaning forward. Pinch the soft part of the nose for at least ten minutes, holding a bowl under the nose to catch any blood. If bleeding persists, repeat at ten-minute intervals. Once the bleeding has stopped, do not allow the child to blow his or her nose.

Splinters: Clean the area with soap and water. Sterilize some tweezers in a flame and gently pull out the splinter along its entry line.

Sprains: Immobilize the area, then apply a cold compress in the form of an ice pack or frozen peas. Apply a wad of cotton wool, secured with a bandage, and keep the limb raised until the pain subsides.

Vomiting: Offer reassurance, wipe the child's face with a cool damp cloth, and encourage him or her to rest quietly in a cool room, with a bowl close by in case vomiting occurs again. Offer small sips of water.

Have to hand: sterile dressings ★ eyebath and sterile water ★ plasters ★ tweezers ★ cotton wool ★ packets of frozen peas ★ bandages

Index

Acknowledgements

We would like to thank Heidi Tibbles, 34 Ridge Street, Watford, Hertfordshire (01923 254609) for making the children's costumes, and Stephanie Spyrakis, Creative Faces, 52a Sutton Road, London N10 1HE (0181 444 4489) for painting their faces. We would also like to thank Party Party, 11 Southampton Road, London NW5 4JS (0171 267 9084) for lending us props, and Charles Bradley for making some of them. Thank you, too, to Rachel Fuller, for helping us out in the office. And last but not least, we would like to say a particularly big thank you to all the following children for having their pictures taken: Anastasia Barker; Miriam Blume; Becky Creber; Emily Creber; Thomas Gage; Lucy Johnson; Adam Lofthouse; Lisa Milner; Yasmin Milner; Peter Milsom; James Moller; Samuel Oladeinde; Lucy Rands; Siân Richards; Sanchez Stokes; Alistair Tweedale; and Edmond Wood. We couldn't have produced this book without them.